LEAP OF FAITH

LEAP OF FAITH

By

NORMAN P. GRUBB

CHRISTIAN LITERATURE CRUSADE
Fort Washington, Pennsylvania 19034

© 1962

CHRISTIAN LITERATURE CRUSADE

CANADA
1440 Mackay Street, Montreal, Quebec
GREAT BRITAIN
The Dean, Alresford, Hampshire
AUSTRALIA
P.O. Box 91, Pennant Hills, N.S.W. 2120
NEW ZEALAND
Box 1688, Auckland, C.1

Also in:
Europe—Africa—South America—India
Philippines—Thailand—New Guinea
Pakistan—Indonesia—Japan
Caribbean Area

This Edition 1971

SBN 87508 — 215 — 7

Printed by Christian Literature Crusade
Fort Washington, Pennsylvania, U.S.A.

CONTENTS

FOREWORD

It came as a surprise to me when the Christian Literature Crusade staff asked me to write the story of the
C.L.C., but I counted it a great privilege. I have been
part of the C.L.C. in spirit since the day of its birth and
have continued in the closest fellowship through the years,
both in heart and often in consultation with many of its
workers, particularly with Ken and Bessie Adams. But
naturally with the wide and rapid world expansion of the
C.L.C., I became out of touch with the details of many
of its activities.

As with the writing of any biography, whether of an
individual or a company of individuals, I believe that
nothing lives like first-hand accounts of personal experience. I have built this testimony on that basis. It is a
testimony, because it is people telling what God is doing,
and doing by common humans. This little book is really
only another chapter, one of thousands upon thousands
through the centuries, added to the book of the Acts of
the Apostles; or, if you like, another verse added to
Hebrews 11.

If I give my personal testimony about it, I must say
that it has absolutely thrilled me to prepare this manuscript. It has not been a chore but a joy. I have fed myself
on what I have been preparing, delighting as I went along
in all the variety of deeply human-divine experiences of
the different workers; human in shrinkings, inadequacies,
temptations to run away, and often very comic situations;

divine in it being all the time the living God Himself clothing Himself in the members of Christ's body, and His strength being made gloriously perfect in their weaknesses. It really is something to see and laugh at the rickety starts of these various launches of faith, and then to see emerging a properly-run literature organization which can meet the commercial world on its own level. Yet the end and aim of it is the bringing of Christ-centered literature to millions of people in many countries. But in doing so, they are always first a company of co-workers whose primary activity and interest is not sales but souls; not a business but a ministry. They are a great commercial organization which never moves away from its "foolish" foundation, walking on the tightrope of faith, in continual dependence on the faithfulness of God for the daily bread of the workers, while using what profits it makes, and the gifts from God's people, for the outpouring of literature to the world.

I think it should be noted that the incidents and experiences in this book are only illustrations of what is happening in similar ways and with other co-workers on every field. It is obvious that among a company of more than 250 literature workers the few must represent the many in a record of this nature. As C.L.C. was born in Britain, the first part of this narrative is naturally centered there, but the story widens out to North America, Australia and all parts of the world.

I wish to acknowledge my gratitude to my co-worker, Miss Mildred McCadden, the one who has taken the heavy end of the typing of the manuscript for the Lord's sake.

"All Thy works shall praise Thee, O Lord; and Thy saints shall bless Thee."

N. P. G.
Fort Washington, Pennsylvania — 1962

1

UNCONSCIOUS PREPARATION

A lad of fourteen, on the way to becoming a tall, broad-shouldered young man with large, capable hands, a crop of crisp, curly hair, and the keen features of a future man of business, was on his way to London. "It was quite a big day for me," he said. "I was answering the newspaper to try and get myself a job. I had four or five appointments lined up. I bought myself a hat for the occasion—one of those famous bowler hats—in order to be a proper city gentleman with bowler hat and umbrella! But in my lack of experience in buying hats, I bought it a size or two too big. There I was racing for the train, and if it hadn't been for my ears, you wouldn't have seen anything but a hat going to the train!"

But there was a background to this young life: a Christian home; a godly mother who had hung as a motto in the home, "that in all things He might have the pre-eminence"; and the boy himself brought to a saving knowledge of the Lord. He knew it very clearly and very definitely at eight years of age. At twelve, through a talk with his missionary sister, a conviction registered in his heart that he had not only been saved, but that there was some purpose for his life in God's work.

The apostle Paul said that God had it all planned out for him, from his birth to his calling; "Who separated me from my mother's womb and called me by His grace," and that certainly included his intervening teen-age years. So, also, with this young lad—Kenneth Adams. How much

hangs on that invisible thread! Watch it unravel, the
working of God's grace in the young responsive heart
making his conscious choices—with God.

Two jobs were offered him, one at a candy factory, ten
hours a day for seventeen shillings and six pence ($2.50)
a week, and one in a paper firm eight hours a day for
fifteen shillings (50¢ less).

"What are you going to do?" asked his mother.

"I'm going to pray about it," he replied, and his mother
prayed too. The choice he made was the paper firm, not
because of the shorter hours but because he was engaged
in Christian work, helping in a young people's meeting
which started at 7 o'clock and he was determined to
keep going in the Lord's work. "If you had asked me
at the time the significance of this choice," recalls Ken
"I wouldn't have known—and for years I didn't. But what
was the difference? One firm was quite a way out of
town, but the one I took was right in the heart of the
City almost within a stone's throw of St. Paul's Cathedral.
At the other side of St. Paul's, prior to World War II,
was Paternoster Row, a whole area where probably sev-
enty-five percent of the evangelical publishing houses and
bookstores were located. I had an hour for lunch, and
would go over to St. Paul's with my sandwiches and eat
them in the courtyard. Then, to while away the other
forty minutes, I would go to Paternoster Row and start
browsing; one day at Pickering and Inglis, another at
Samuel Bagster's, another at Marshall, Morgan and Scott,
another at the London Bible House, etc. Quite unconsciously there was being instilled into my teen-age mind
and heart, an interest in literature. I wouldn't like to say
I was a bookworm, but I was certainly interested in books.
More than that, I found interest in talking about books
to other young people back in my home church.

"That led on to the beginning of a bookstore ministry
in my home town in just a private capacity. I began to
see real possibilities in working for myself instead of being

in business for somebody else, and working in a type of job that would have some sort of spiritual ministry in it."

A vacation spent with missionaries in Spain deepened the sense of missionary call, but on the other hand business began to pull. "I had gone into the business world with this Christian bookstore," continues Ken. "Things began to go quite happily and successfully, so much so that after the first Christmas I moved with my mother and sisters into second premises with living quarters above, in Westcliff-on-Sea. As a result of this second move, with sales, and therefore money beginning to increase, the business 'bump' in me began to come to the fore. I soon saw possibilities of enlargement, particularly along the line of legal stationery, documents for offices, etc. As a matter of fact I was now looking at a third location, bigger and offering more possibilities.

"Then one night, in the quietness of my room, the Lord challenged me and said, 'Ken, didn't you say that you believed you were going to be a missionary one day?'

" 'Yes, that's right, Lord, I did.'

" 'Well, what about it my son?'

" 'Well, what about it, Lord?'

"And so the argument went back and forth, and I was suddenly conscious again of two ways. Was this now the Lord's time for another decision—a decision to plunge more deeply into business, perhaps getting more involved financially? Or was this the time to face up to the challenge of full-time missionary service? The visit to Spain was brought to my mind again. One Sunday night after the services were over I sat in front of the fire and said to mother, 'What would you think of me if I sold this business?'—just right out like that.

" 'Why?' she asked.

"Then I began to tell her how the Lord had been speaking to my heart and I was feeling that perhaps I ought to prepare for Christian service. Again, that gracious mother of mine said, 'Well, son, if this is God's word to you, go ahead and do it.' "

An old man of seventy took over the bookstore while Ken went off to the Faith Mission in Scotland for Bible training. Even in the take-over of the bookstore, another link in the chain was forged, for this man had as his assistant a young man named John Whittle, who was a pastor of a small church. "But John wasn't fully satisfied spiritually. He felt there was something else. The particular group he was with was quite circumscribed, and he felt there were other good Christians 'out there.' God began to speak to his heart as he was reading a book concerning a particular mission. The message of this book was what he was thirsting for, he felt. So he went to visit that mission expecting to find the things recorded in this book; instead he found a coldness there, an orderliness, a ten-minute chat type of thing. The flow of spiritual life he had read about in the book was lacking. He went away disillusioned. Continuing his reading he came across another, Eva Stuart Watt's book, *Floods on Dry Ground*. 'This is what I'm after, this is it. I'll try again,' he said. This time he went to the Worldwide Evangelization Crusade Headquarters in Upper Norwood. Here, we say it humbly and to the glory of God, he found something very much nearer that for which his heart was searching. This led him to face up to the implications of full-time missionary service, and then to a definite link with this group, convinced that this was the place for which God had been preparing him. There were plenty of disillusionments, plenty of things that weren't in the book even in this mission. And yet, John is still in the Crusade today." You may wonder what the call of John Whittle had to do with the birth of the Christian Literature Crusade, but that will be apparent later on.

Meanwhile, because of the Civil War in Spain the door for Ken Adams to missionary service there closed. So what next? Just a thread of guidance, and how much hung on it. "The Lord finally led me down to Cornwall in the southwest of England. My contact had come through a summer campaign during Faith Mission days, as four of us preached the gospel night after night. During the course of that campaign an ex-major of the British Army and his young wife, who were touring in Perthshire, Scotland, threw in their lot with us for a week. One of my colleagues, who had been a down - and - outer and drunkard, gave his testimony the first night. The old major strutted up to him afterwards and exclaimed, 'That was a jolly fine testimony. You know, I was an old stinker like you once!' Later the good major wrote and told me that God had been blessing down in Cornwall in some Methodist churches in quite a measure of revival. He also said that some recent converts needed Bible teaching, and knowing of my interest in this type of ministry, asked if I could come down. He didn't realize that his letter reached me when I had come to a crossroads in my life. It was his letter which directed my steps to Cornwall.

"And here we suddenly get romantic because this is where . . . ."

2

ONE COMPLEMENTS THE OTHER

A young Cornish woman appears on the scene, not a
literature enthusiast like Ken, but one with a tender
heart for God and people, one who, side by side with
Ken, could bring the compassion of Christ, so essential
in community living, to the needs of their fellow workers.
Bessie Adams, then Bessie Miners, was born into a large
family of twelve children. "We had a very godly father
whose life spoke much of the love of Christ to me as a
child," recalls Bessie. "He was a great reader. Although
a busy fisherman, he used to take time out to read to us
Christian fiction and books such as *Pilgrim's Progress*.
This gave me a great love for Christian literature and for
reading.

"At the age of fourteen I began working in a grocery,
drapery and footwear store where a very godly young
woman made quite an impact on my life. Two years
later I came to know Christ as my personal Saviour. It
happened this way. God was moving in our village and
in our Methodist Church. The Spirit was working might-
ily. Each night in special evangelistic services I saw the
old-fashioned penitent rail filled with men and women
seeking Christ. One particular night they were singing
that lovely hymn, 'Have You Any Room for Jesus?' When
they came to the last verse,

'Room for pleasure, room for business,
But for Christ the crucified,
Not a place that He can enter,
In your heart for which He died?'

the Holy Spirit spoke deeply to my heart. I turned to the girl next to me and said, 'I am going up to the penitent rail.' As I knelt at that mercy seat, God did a real work in my heart. I shall never forget it. In all the years that have followed, I have never doubted my soul's salvation. To me it was a tremendous thing. I was turned from the power of satan to God. I was a new creature in Christ Jesus, and I have never lost the wonder of that memorable night.

"From then on the Lord began to give me opportunities for Christian service. Once a week we met in a little Methodist class meeting where we shared our testimonies of what the Lord had done for us and something of our battles during the week. I also sang in the choir, visited the sick and helped in open-air work. Each Sunday I taught a young women's Bible class. As we studied the Word of God, it became very real and precious to my own heart. I was quite content in my little home town witnessing for Christ and busy in Christian activities. As time went on, God spoke to my heart about a deeper walk with Him.

"During another series of special services a young fellow from Ireland challenged us about a life wholly committed to God. I saw something new of a life which really counted for God. One night during the campaign I made a total commitment of my life to the Lord and gave Him all that I had and all that I ever hoped to be. A week or two later I was reading the magazine of the Friends Evangelistic Band, *Caravan News.* Here I caught something of the spiritual need in the villages of England where often there was practically no vital gospel witness. God spoke to my heart and said, 'Bessie, that is where I want you. I want you to leave business. You've been making lots of money for your boss. Now I want you to go out and win souls for Me.' That evening I had a battle. Praise God, He won. I was very fond of all my dear family and the Lord brought that Scripture to my mind,

'He that loveth father or mother more than me is not worthy of me.' "

For some years following this, Bessie worked in the villages of England. She returned home due to the illness of her father, and while home was asked to conduct evangelistic services in some of the nearby villages. Many had been praying for years for the salvation of their families and now felt the Holy Spirit indicating this to be the time of harvest. "It came as a great surprise to me," relates Bessie, "for I had never preached a sermon in my life. How wonderfully the Holy Spirit worked. I realized the truth of that verse I have taken throughout my life, 'Not by might, nor by power, but by my Spirit, saith the Lord.' It wasn't to be by great preaching. The Holy Ghost was brooding over those villages. For miles around, the blessed gospel hymns were being sung. The news quickly spread that revival had broken out. Conviction and repentance were much in evidence. Scores came to Christ. Mrs. Flint, wife of a retired Army major, was helping me in these services. One day, she said to me, 'You know, Bess, these converts need building up in the Word of God. I was in Scotland recently and met four young fellows. One, in particularly, is well versed in the Scriptures. His name is Kenneth Adams. Do you think if he came down, there would be a place for him in ministering to these young converts?' I said, 'Oh yes, that would be wonderful.'

"And so Ken came down . . . ."

3

THE DAWN OF A CALL

After marriage and some months of Bible teaching and evangelism in the Cornish villages, they went to London looking to the Lord for the next step. They had a choice of two. The one they made established them by conviction in a principle which had great importance for the future.

"We went to a good friend of Bessie's," recalls Ken Adams, "George Fox, founder and leader of the Friends Evangelistic Band, with which Bessie had been working. This group, an interdenominational mission for evangelism in the villages, would send workers to do visitation and try to reopen closed chapels. Prior to this we had made contact with Mr. Nash who was quite high up in political affairs in Britain. He was an uncle of Sir Hugh Foot, a former governor of Jamaica. Mr. Nash invited us to become the superintendent of the Plymouth City Mission and with a good salary. We would have a home provided for us, a luxury we had not yet enjoyed as a young married couple. All our worldly goods were in the back of our little Austin car, which was not much more than a matchbox on wheels! I had never been a smoker except in that car — plenty of fumes all the time! We prayed about this offer. At the time we were staying with dear friends of ours in London, Harold and Ethel Hogbin. They have stood with us over the years and now advised us, 'Ken and Bessie, this is obviously God's answer. You didn't seek it, the letter came out of the blue.' Yet, after we had spent some days quietly considering the proposition, we concluded: 'No, it is not for us. God has called us to a life of faith, not a paid salary type of life.' We had nothing against salaries and don't to this day. However, God had launched us from the beginning into a faith ministry and we felt that that was to remain one of the marks of our future service, whatever it was to be. That was clear from the Lord. Accordingly we turned down the City Mission offer and went into village work with Mr. Fox and his Evangelistic Band.

"It was tough work, but the Lord blessed. A few came to salvation. Quickly we saw a place for literature and organized a booktable. That was where my earlier interest in literature began to come back into the visible. In the summer months we conducted tent campaigns. The burden to get out into villages with literature, instead of just having it on a bookstall, grew with us. But something else happened. In these villages we were challenged by a different kind of literature campaign. As we visited the people in their homes, we found the literature of Jehovah's Witnesses, and we became troubled about it. Everywhere people would show us copies of the books they had purchased, not from the city bookstore, but from a 'Publisher' who had stood right on the doorstep and poured out a sales story, persisting until finally a purchase was made. Now we were really disturbed. We were challenged, and have continually been, by these cults and by Communists. They display a fervor, a zeal, and a missionary activity of outstanding quality.

"We prayed much about this. It was a real burden with us, but quite frankly, we weren't prepared for the way God was about to answer. I had a funny feeling—I don't know whether Bess did or not—that somewhere or other along the line we were going to get involved. My particular burden was: why didn't all these preaching points in the F.E.B. have literature and bookstalls, and then take this literature from door to door? As we chatted it over, we said, 'Let's just commit it to the Lord and leave it. If it is of the Lord, He must make either Rev. George Banks or Mr. George Fox write a letter and specifically ask us to do this very thing we are talking about.' We had no sooner come to that conclusion, than, within a couple of days a letter marked 'confidential' came to our door. We didn't even have to open that letter. We looked at each other and said, 'You know what this is don't you?' Sure enough, it was from George Banks, written on behalf of George Fox. They had just had a board meeting. Would we set up a literature program for them? We didn't have to pray about that request. We were caught! Frankly there was a measure of disappointment in our hearts. This was not quite the way we wanted things to go. Our hope was that we could remain in direct evangelism but perhaps help in some way to get a literature program organized. We did not want to get too involved— Bess perhaps more particularly than myself. I had this business trait in me. Bess's heart and soul were in evangelism, and it was a much tougher proposition for her. But there was one condition attached, which again was the Lord keeping us free for the future. The Board was not willing for it to be a department of the Friends Evangelistic Band. There were some who felt very strongly that literature was necessary, but others couldn't see it. We were to set it up as individuals and use the F.E.B. as our main source of distribution. 'But how can we start?' we asked. 'We don't have any money.'

" 'Well,' George Banks said, as we talked the matter over later, 'we do have £100* in our account which is earmarked for another project. We are not able to use it for the moment, so we will make it available to you, if you undertake to pay it back as the literature work prospers.' So that's how the matter was settled and within a few weeks the work was started.

"Off in our little matchbox of a car I went to London,

(*To calculate British pounds in dollars, multiply by four to give an approximate value £1=$4) first to Oliphants. I was invited into the warehouse and began my ordering: twenty of this, twenty of that, and twenty-five of another! I didn't have any codes for buying in those days! We loaded that car until it didn't have any springs. It went home on the axles! But we were soon back for more. To publisher after publisher we went, and it was amazing how these firms believed our story. There was no question about paying cash on the nail; they just believed our story and willingly gave us their usual business credit terms. So we built up the stock and went into action in some rooms in Colchester. We set up a book-room in the largest of the rooms. A smaller room to the side was our living quarters; there was no gas installation, so we cooked on a little oil stove. It was also the packing room, office and everything else as well. Upstairs were two more rooms. One was used as a storeroom and the other was our bedroom. It had a sloping roof and I couldn't stand up straight. In winter the snow came in through the skylight. It was a great life! A narrow spiral staircase was the only access to these rooms. I found I couldn't get the bedstead up the stairs. We got it jammed and couldn't move it one way or the other, so I got a hacksaw and cut it in two! From then on it was a rattling good bed to be sure!"

"Those were days of real struggle for me," Bessie adds. "Little did I dream what God had in store. I had a tremendous inner battle in my own heart. My burden was to get out where I could touch lives and do evangelistic work. God had blessed and by His grace and mercy we had seen what He could do in revival, but here we were shut away in these little upstairs rooms and a tiny kitchen. Funds were limited and we had very little furniture. We lived pretty primitively. The enemy used to taunt me and say, 'Look here, Bess. Ken really doesn't love you. Watch the birds of the air; they make their nests and provide for their mate and their young. But look how you are living!' How he tortured my mind.

But, hallelujah, God came through. Ken was very busy packing parcels of literature which were sent out to the village evangelists. Soon we were encouraged by hearing of the blessing God was pleased to pour out through these books and literature. Now, instead of the Jehovah's Witnesses having all the field, here we were. Young converts and people living in the remote parts of England could now get Bibles and other Christian books that would build them up in the faith, brought to them in their homes. This brought great joy to our hearts."

"This is where we began the literature ministry," Ken continues. "Little did we realize then the far-reaching scope this work was destined to have. Incidentally, we found that this little living room was actually C. H. Spurgeon's bedroom when he was a student at a nearby academy. It is interesting that later on C.L.C. in Britain purchased the property of the colportage department of C. H. Spurgeon's ministry. So there have been two links with Spurgeon, the great prince of preachers.

"After we had spent about eight months in the upstairs rooms, the Lord indicated that we should move. Better premises were needed to enable us to reach the people of the city, so we began a search for property. (We've been at this ever since!) It wasn't difficult to find premises. Britain was now at war with Germany and people were beginning to leave the cities in search of some safer place. Finally we came across quite a suitable building in a good location. It was three or four doors away from the main bus depot and therefore many people from the villages passed our door. Here we were—beginning a program with only borrowed money and now new expenses. But God had given us the word. With confidence in our hearts and a little bit of sanctified 'cheek,' we went to see what could be done. The owner told us the price would be £2 a week. That was far beyond what we could dare to undertake, so we made a business deal with him.

" 'Look,' we said, 'the war is on and, who knows, we

might get bombed out before long. The best we can offer you is £1 a week.'

"He looked at me aghast and said, 'Are you serious?'

" 'Yes,' I said, 'I am!'

"Reluctantly he decided that this was better than nothing, and agreed to let us have the place and we went home rejoicing. We had been paying seven shillings ($1) a week for the upstairs rooms, so you see we'd taken quite a sizeable leap. What is more we now faced the stocking and furnishing of a three-storied building.

"We couldn't afford a moving company and, in any case, didn't have much furniture; so we borrowed a handcart and hauled the furniture around to 17 St. Johns Street. All we had was a bed, a table and a couple of chairs. These wouldn't go far in five or six rooms.

"Naturally Bessie was concerned and asked, 'What are we going to do about furniture?'

"I replied, 'There's an auction sale up the road every week. I'll go and see what's there.'

"I wouldn't like to say this was the Lord's doings on our behalf, but certainly the timing was of the Lord. The war was on but there had never been so much as a bomb dropped or an enemy plane across the coast of Britain at night. People were beginning to wonder what sort of war we were fighting. Then on Tuesday we had our first night air raid of World War II. The next morning I was at the sale room. There was only a handful of people, whereas normally there would be two or three hundred. They had to go through with their selling because more furniture would be coming the following week. Consequently things sold for a mere song. As a matter of fact, several times they had difficulty in selling the particular lot and the auctioneer would say, 'All right, put the next lot with it.' I had been around the sale room and had my eye on certain things. There was a nice settee with two easy chairs, a useful sideboard and many other similar items. It wasn't long before my head began to nod and the purchases to pile up! When I got back to Bessie and began to itemize the things that had been purchased, they came to just about £2. I think we had fifteen or twenty chairs (just regular straight-backed ones, all odds and ends) for which we paid about two pence (2c) each. The settee and two easy chairs cost us fifteen shillings ($3). After several years of hard wear this same three-piece suite was put back into the sale room and produced £21!

"Now the question was, what were we going to do about paying for it? We had to get the furniture out of the auction room by Friday. The Lord had the answer the very next day. The previous Sunday we had been to dinner with a local family and in the course of conversation got onto the famous subject of weekly rations—how were we getting on with two ounces of butter, only one pound of sugar and no eggs?

"Bessie commented, 'We have a bit of trouble with the sugar because Ken likes plenty of it in his tea!' It was just a passing comment like that, and we went on talking about other things. Thursday morning one of the ladies was in the bookstore. She handed a small package to me and said, 'Would you give this to your good wife?' Just as she turned to leave, and with a sort of twinkle in her eye, she added, 'If you're a good boy, maybe you can have some.' That raised my suspicion, and sure enough when we opened it there was a two-pound package of sugar— and on top of the package two pound notes! We hadn't said a word at the meal table on Sunday about our plans to buy furniture the following Wednesday. The Lord used this, and many a similar experience, to confirm us in this policy of simple faith and trust for every need, both personal and for the work. Many times since then faith has been honored, sometimes with £2, sometimes £200 or $2,000, as the work of the Lord has advanced around the world. Of course at this time we had no idea where God was leading. One thing we did know, we were not to go into a paid salary type of ministry, but to launch into a daily trusting of Him for our needs. This was to become a basic policy.

"The store was now opened for business and, praise the Lord, for the first time in our literature ministry, we took in more than £10 in one week. In the little room upstairs it had been £3 one week, £5 another, but never to £10. Then the Lord began to bring in the people. We had far greater contacts in this ground floor store than we did in the upstairs room. Soon it was our joy to lead souls to Christ and fellowship with God's people in the things of the Spirit.

"Colchester is a large military town, the second largest in England. This meant there were plenty of soldiers around, not only British soldiers, but Australians, New Zealanders, Canadians and Americans. Bessie's particular burden was evangelism, and it wasn't long before she suggested, 'You know, Ken, God has been speaking to me and I'm troubled about all these soldiers milling around here. We ought to do something about it.'"

The result was a decision to rent the Friends Meeting House each Sunday night and open a canteen. It was to be a faith launch. "And I tell you," says Bessie, "hungry fellows can eat well. There was one lad in particular who was a rough diamond. The Lord had saved him from a pretty wild life, and he kept coming for fellowship. He was one of the first to join us and used to call me 'Mrs.' 'Mrs., you need something,' he said on one occasion, 'you'll need a bit of "this" to help you out with the refreshments'; and that dear fellow put in my hand two pound notes, just crumpled up like little bits of dirty paper. Bill's gift was the first the Lord sent us to begin buying the refreshments. Saturday by Saturday I would go to the confectioner's shop and, in spite of rationing, come home with trays full of buns and cakes. Every week the Lord provided. I suppose we're not exaggerating when we say that thousands of soldiers came under the sound of the gospel through Bill's witness. Others soon joined the team, Americans, Canadians, young men from different countries, and God knitted us together in the Spirit. Some would go down to the main street and invite the soldiers into the gospel meeting. We'd have the team lined up from street to street so that the boys wouldn't miss their way, and then I would stand at the top of the stairs and give them a welcome. We never had an ordinary kind of service; indeed, I think I was forever spoiled for the more formal hymn, prayer and a reading type of meeting. These were spontaneous in the Spirit. I'll never forget the first meeting we had. There were mainly men of the Pioneer Corps attending and most hadn't been to a service since they were children. Informally we said, 'Now fellows, we're going to sing a few hymns, and let's have some of your favorites.' Do you know the first hymn one of those men chose? He said, 'I'd like for us to sing' (and this is why we should never underestimate Sunday School work amongst children), 'Yes, Jesus loves me!' Another chose, 'Where is my wandering boy tonight?' The Spirit of God came down, and again and again we had the joy of leading men to the Lord, sometimes almost in groups."

4

BIRTH OUT OF TRAVAIL

There are great moments, and there are lesser moments in our lives. The lesser are stages on our pioneer journey, often rugged enough, to the land of discovery, the land of our destiny, the "works before ordained that we should walk in them." We have been tracing those intervening years in the lives of Ken and Bessie Adams. Now came the great moment of their life's calling. Yet all happened so unconsciously, so almost incidentally, that the great moment, as we look back, resembles merely the fitting of a key piece into a jigsaw puzzle.

At this time Ken and Bessie came to a situation with the F.E.B. which doubtless gave pain to both sides. Because of Ken's business instinct, and perhaps some over-zealous suggestions of business reorganization not acceptable from such a neophyte, the brethren in the F.E.B. felt that it would be best to give the Adamses their complete independence and freedom to go forward as led in the future. It hurt. These things do hurt. However, between them and the brethren of the F.E.B. that hurt has long since been swallowed up in the love of Christ, and the F.E.B. have rejoiced in God's new way for their former colleagues. Since then, indeed, the Adamses themselves have had to know the pain of such partings from fellow workers at different times, and the ever-pressing questions: was it really our fault or theirs? But the beauty of failures, by God's wonderful alchemy, is that they become the breeding ground for a holy determination to learn and practice the secret of the "wisdom which is from above," pure, peaceable, gentle, easy to be entreated. Constantly to replace the "wisdom from beneath," of envying and strife, by this higher wisdom, and to find the oneness of mind when all "speak the same thing," as well as the basic oneness of heart—these are secrets the C.L.C. has been learning.

Yet, marvelously enough, even painful partings, whatever the rights or wrongs may be, are directed by God to His larger ends. Without this severance from F.E.B. there would be, humanly speaking, no C.L.C. today. Perhaps the truth is that partings are not always wrong, just as physical life is based on cell-division; but the spirit in which the parting takes place is the crucial factor.

"By the beginning of 1941 the bookstore had legally become our own property," says Ken Adams. "We had also paid back the £100 which had been borrowed. Yet we knew that this bookstore didn't really belong to us; it had not been our money which had brought it into being. We had merely served the Lord in this way. Now what was to happen to it, we asked ourselves.

"Among the mission magazines we were reading was *World Conquest*, the publication of the Worldwide Evangelization Crusade. Soon after the war started, the W.E.C. was led to consider a widening of their home front program, turning by faith the apparent frustration of war into a challenge to advance. Part of the advance was a plan for regional headquarters. Twelve were planned, and their artist, Charlton Smith, had prepared a map of the British Isles showing the various cities and areas in which these regional centers would be opened. We noticed that there was to be a regional center in East Anglia. The city chosen was Norwich, some sixty miles from Colchester. The Lord used this to lead us another step forward. In our judgement, Colchester was as good a center as Norwich—both were located in East Anglia. We decided to write to the W.E.C. and tell them they would be welcome to establish their regional headquarters with us in Colchester. We would provide a room for the worker they would send and it wouldn't cost them anything.

"By that time, our good friend John Whittle was back in the picture. How much was now to come out of that slender link with him in those earlier days! After his eighteen months in the W.E.C. headquarters, the revelation of God's purposes had become clear. In the regional program of advance, John was to be the spearhead of the troops. He was to go in turn to each of these areas and try to establish the base of operation. So it happened that he came to Colchester to the same friends who had provided the two pounds of sugar and the two pound notes. When we heard this, we immediately phoned and asked them to tell John that we would like to see him.

"We met in the afternoon, and spent some time reminiscing. Finally John said, 'Well, I hear you want to see me. What's on your mind?' We told him how God had been speaking to us regarding this regional headquarters' plan and that if, in any way, we could fit in, we were keen to do so. 'That's very interesting,' said John, 'but I know that already! Sitting at the dinner table with the Crawleys, the moment they mentioned your name the Lord witnessed to my heart, "That's the couple you're looking for."

"A few weeks later, John had been able to arrange some meetings for Norman Grubb, Secretary of the W.E.C., and Leslie Sutton, his assistant. The morning after the meetings, these men came to have a chat with us. By this time, of course, the news had been passed on to them, and we now told in more detail how the Lord had led, wondering what exactly would come out of it. As far as we could see there was only one problem—what to do with the bookstore. We were willing to sell it or to employ someone to run it, which would then leave us free to do the outside contact work. As the work had started as a minis-

try and not a business, and had had the evident seal of
the Lord on it, we could not feel it right that the bookstore should now be closed. While we discussed the pros
and cons of the problem, the word of light came again in
one of those flashes of inspiration: Norman Grubb
answered our problem by saying, 'Indeed not! Close it
down? Why, we ought to have these Christian bookstores
scattered all over the place—sort of "spiritual Woolworths"
up and down the country.'

If God had been preparing the Adamses, He had also
been preparing the W.E.C. Two of its members who
have already been mentioned, Leslie Sutton and Charlton
Smith, had been constantly stressing through the years
that this was the era of world literacy, and that W.E.C.
should not only be an evangelistic society in the sense of
preaching the gospel to the unevangelized, but should also
develop a definite literature ministry. Because this constantly reiterated challenge had gradually sunk into my
consciousness, it came as a natural (though supernatural)
response when Ken made the condition that the bookstore
should be retained if he came into W.E.C. This would
normally be out of keeping with our W.E.C. regional
activities: "No, don't close it down. Duplicate it all over
the place!" Such an idea was also possible, because God
had always led W.E.C. to remain flexible, not bound to
fixed methods, but ready to jump in whenever a new
door of ministry opened.

Yet how much comes from what is apparently so little!
The "spiritual Woolworth" statement was almost a joke—
yet not a joke. Behind it lay the purpose of God which
has blossomed out into the present-day worldwide C.L.C.
God in his wisdom knew how to make this marriage between these two—one sold out for evangelism by literature,
and the other an organization with a world vision, free
and flexible enough to give a helping hand in establishing
the literature ministry on a world scale.

And so the great moment had come. Not by the normal

procedure of completing official papers, meeting an official board, and so forth, but by the meeting of hearts and minds in the flash point of revelation, demonstrated by these twenty-one years to have been a light and voice from heaven.

"Well, that was taking us a lot further than we'd ever dreamed of," continues Ken. "We were thinking only in terms of representing the W.E.C. and keeping this one bookstore alive. When we found that there was such hearty enthusiasm to this little scheme, we watched to see what God would do. It was immediately apparent that some additional workers would need to come in if we were going to be released for traveling. From the beginning it was agreed that personnel would be called 'workers,' because we would not be 'employing' anyone.

"On their way back to London the following day, the party stopped at Chelmsford, a city about twenty-two miles away. When Rubi (as Norman Grubb is called by his African name in W.E.C. circles) once gets an idea in his head, he's all enthusiastic about it and drops everything else! During the tea interval at the Chelmsford meetings, Rubi was talking with different friends and eventually came to have something to eat. By this time there was only a small table left, occupied by Mr. and Mrs. Whybrow, the W.E.C. prayer battery representatives for Chelmsford. With these new bookstore ideas uppermost in his mind, it wasn't long before Rubi said, 'By the way, do you know the Adamses at Colchester?' They said they didn't, but their son, Humphrey, knew them quite well because he played an accordian and helped them in their soldiers' meetings. Then Rubi told the story of the proposed new bookstore outreach throughout the country. 'Now,' he said, 'we've got to see God bring in some workers.' Rubi didn't have the slightest idea he was talking to possible prospective workers."

"We went from that meeting with a strange feeling in our hearts that God was speaking to us," recalls Mr.

Whybrow, "although we did not mention it to each other until the following Monday evening. For two years previously we had felt that God would lead us out into full-time service, and this now seemed possible seeing our son and daughter had gone into Bible school. We learned long afterwards that they had been praying to this end also. So we wrote to Mr. Grubb offering for W.E.C. work in the bookshop at Colchester, and started on the trail—for what? Little did we know we were to be 'foundation members' of a Crusade which was to have such an impact on England and almost every other country in the world."

By the time the Whybrows (Pa and Ma Why, as they are called in the crusade family) were ready to join with the Adamses, a move was made to a larger house which became the East Anglia Regional Headquarters. Here they pooled all their furniture and lived as one family; others soon being added to their number.

5

PIONEERING ON A SHOESTRING

The early pioneer days were a real testing for each who joined. As Bessie Adams says, "Those days must have been a real trial for dear Ma and Pa Why. Here we were, just a young couple, immature in many ways; whereas they had run their own home for years and also had two grown children. Yet God had put us together. I will ever praise God for the grace, patience and love of the dear Whybrows."

Pa Why had his tests in the store. "The early days were for me a terrific testing time," he recounts, "although through it all I had a peace and satisfaction in my heart, because I knew He was somewhere in the situation. After a week or two I was left alone to run the shop. My general knowledge of business and business methods was fairly good, but I had no knowledge of, or training in, Bible and book selling. There I was: errand boy, shop cleaner, packer, shop assistant, literary and spiritual consultant, and managing director—each position receiving the same salary! After one particularly difficult day I got down before the Lord to ask Him why I was there. How could I possibly make any contribution in this way to worldwide evangelization? It was then I received my first lesson in practical obedience to the call of God. There were to be no 'if's,' 'whys,' 'hows' or 'buts' in my service to Him. This was His business. All He asked of me was to get on with it, and so I did. Early in 1942 the enemy made his big personal attack. Ma Why was taken seriously ill, which eventually led to a major operation. All our planning seemed to go wrong. Were we right in leaving home, our work at the local Gospel Mission and the security of secular employment? Was God really in what now began to assume more and more the aspect of a mad adventure? Yes, indeed He was in it! Daily He gave the assurance in our hearts. Since those days the trail has led on to include seven years' leadership in the C.L.C. These years of the C.L.C. history, and our part in it, are most certainly the Lord's doings and marvelous in our eyes!"

Housekeeping by faith and on a communal basis was a new experience, especially as numbers increased. "You can well imagine as the household grew," says Bessie again, "with Phil and Mim Booth, Leslie and Nora Fitton and others joining us, we needed to see God supply in a greater way for our kitchen purse. The Whybrows and Ken and I had already covenanted with God that we wouldn't take any funds at all out of the business. Indeed, as He enabled, we made it our responsibility to put something into the kitchen purse. It was wonderful. He never failed. Ken or Pa would often have preaching appointments and be given a little bit of money. Each time they came home they gladly put their contribution into the purse. If one week Ma didn't have any money, Ken and I would have the privilege of supplying. If we didn't have anything, then perhaps Ma and Pa would be able to contribute. Others also would help as the Lord enabled them. This was true when God added Mim and Phil Booth to us. Their first contribution was £5. To me that was a fortune! And for the next few weeks, sure enough, here would come five more pounds. But the time came when dear Mim and Phil didn't have £5 to put in, and God took them through a deep walk in this life of faith. My, how they walked it! Once when they were without money for bus fare for their daughter Lois, Mim was cleaning the settee, and there found some money, which was sufficient for the car fare to school.

"There were other ways in which our needs were met. One weekend Ken, our daughter Margaret, and I visited our Chatham bookstore. Returning on Monday afternoon, we had difficulty in getting to our house because the German planes had been over bombing. Four bombs had fallen on our neighborhood and several streets were practically demolished. Ma and Pa Why immediately invited the grocer and his family, who lived a few doors from us, into our home because their premises had been badly damaged. They came gladly and brought all the groceries with them! They were not Christians, but as we sought to live Christ before them, we had the joy of seeing Mrs. Groves and the son born of the Spirit of God. Some years later, Mr. Groves also was saved. In due time, the store was repaired and the Groves returned to business. Each week we would get our groceries from their store. Often, to save time, we would place our order and leave it with sufficient money for payment. They would then get it together at their convenience. Many times we would find the pound note or thirty shillings, tucked back into the basket along with the receipted bill. And so, again and again God used these dear friends to help supply our needs."

Mrs. Whybrow adds, "Instead of helping to run a book shop as I had thought, the Lord cornered me and for five years I did the cooking and catering for a growing family. During this time Bessie and I learned many lessons in sharing together, waiting upon God for our daily bread. By this time our family had grown to fifteen adults and six children. Many times we emptied our purse together and enjoyed the spending together, with the thrill of seeing our loving Heavenly Father provide our daily needs. Truly we can say, 'He faileth not.' "

Philip and Miriam Booth, who joined the household in 1944, went through the mill like the rest as we have seen already.

"Really our contact with C.L.C. came about by mistake," Phil said. "The town in which we were living, Newark near Nottingham, was put by W.E.C. into the area under the supervision of Ken and Bessie Adams. In actual fact, it was really in another area, but Ken and Bessie, hearing we were running periodic meetings in our home, asked if they could come along. These were memorable visits and through them the Lord gradually made clear what His mind was for us. We had sought to get to India with W.E.C., but in war days a family could not be accepted for that field. I was director and secretary of quite a big manufacturing concern, which had some 400 employees, and we naturally had quite a nice home. Being in a military training area, we felt led to use our home for house meetings and prayer meetings, Bible studies and hospitality ad lib. As a result the furnishings began to show signs of wear and tear. But the results of these efforts were most rewarding. Scores found Christ as Saviour and some, after military duty was completed, went into fulltime Christian service in different parts of the world. We keep in touch with many of them to this day.

"When it became clear to us that God was calling us out, it was a question of 'To what?' Mim knew immediately; but I must say I struggled quite a lot and for a solid two weeks the battle was on. I was quite prepared to go to the uttermost parts of the earth as a missionary, but to come into this literature work which was just beginning in the W.E.C. was quite another matter. And, of course, there was no overseas work. As far as we could see, we would be leaving our home and job to do, in another home which wouldn't be ours, more or less the same work except, of course, with the additional ministry of the bookstore. However, in the end, the Lord won by His grace and we volunteered. We had a mental impression that we were just going down to Colchester for about two weeks to have a look at things, and then we would be moving off somewhere. As for running a book shop—well, frankly we just hadn't a clue. I suppose that's why we thought that a fortnight might be sufficient.

"When we arrived in Colchester, we were taken upstairs to the top floor, and Bessie very graciously apologized for the room being what it was. She knew something of our home, but this was the best that could be provided at the moment. I must give you some impression of that room in order that you may understand at least one aspect of our battle during those days. It was an attic room. There was just one window at one end, and the doorway was quite low. It meant that both Mim and myself had to bow the neck every time we went in, and once inside I personally wasn't able to stand up straight except in between the beams! (Phil is 6' 2"). When I walked in the room I had to huddle, limping along to miss the beams as I went. At one end, there was a bed for Mim and myself. At the other, were two beds for the children, David at the time six, and Lois two and one-half. Some enthusiast had painted the walls a vivid aquamarine blue. There was just one little gas bracket that served as a light for the whole room. This was so poor that Mim and I had to stand underneath the light in order to read our Bibles together when we had our devotions. The bed! Well, I've learned to sleep in all kinds since, but the whole time I was there, frankly, I was glad to get up, and if you knew me, you would understand that that means quite a lot.

"It wasn't long before the psychological factor began to work, and the children were in trouble through tension. We saw we had to try to make up to them, so we used to get up into that little room after the midday meal and love them and try to create a kind of nest atmosphere, even if there weren't many feathers in the nest! And no doubt throughout the whole of this period we must have been a great test to the grace of the other folk. But we didn't understand that too much at the time. We saw all the 'clay feet' that were to be seen, which is often the experience of candidates, and I think the most trying factor of the whole thing was that nothing developed for us in the way of ministry. The best part of the sixteen months we were there, I packed parcels. That was my main job, in the cold and damp basement, often with fingers cracked open a little bit by the winter weather.

"System just didn't exist in those days and, having just come from a fairly efficient job, I was inclined to be critical. On one occasion I looked across at Pa Why as he did his bookkeeping and said, 'Do you call that bookkeeping, Pa?' You see, I'd been trained as an accountant, among other things. He looked at me very patiently and said, 'Well, Phil, later on you'll understand.' And, of course, I did. As for Mim, she did housework primarily. I myself did a bit of scrubbing for quite a number of months. I had done it before and have done it since, but the rub is, to have that sort of job and no prospect of ever becoming missionaries. And I can tell you there were some tears shed (as Mim said, 'often adding my tears to the water in the bucket').

"Then the children fell ill. Our money was comparatively little, because we had given most of it away before we came into the work. So we just laid our hands on the children and asked God to heal them. And He did. He healed them wonderfully as a rule. Now, with the kids ill, not having a job in one sense, suffering the inner frustrations of this set-up, tired in body and mind, not to mention spirit, our home was in the background all the time. We had visited it occasionally, and it doesn't need much imagination to sense something of the battle we had. One night things were really low. The children were ill, and we hadn't any money. We were absolutely at a deep end (had been for some time) with the shame of not being able to put anything into the housekeeping pool. We were really in the dumps. We sort of touched bottom. When we knelt for our devotions, we told the Lord we just didn't know what He was doing. All we knew was that He had brought us there and that, by His grace, we'd stay.

"Outwardly things did not take a change for the better. During that time of battle, after we had touched bottom, the Lord did come through with many encouragements. Our son, David, was saved and gave testimony to the Lord's dealings with him. We began to have the principle of faith burned into us. Often we had not a penny at all, yet somehow or other the witness of the Lord was that He would supply, and we maintained our stand.

"Also we used to have some great times of fun in Colchester. This was a kind of safety valve. We used to roudy about quite a lot. The house was somewhat secluded, so we could do that sort of thing without up-setting the neighborhood particularly. I won't waste time relating the kind of things we did, but I can tell you some of them were quite wild. And we had some real laughs, which somehow or other helped keep us sane, I really believe. The Lord also had His joke with us from time to time, such as when Ken and Pa Why brought back from London Headquarters a large sack of beans, which we found to be riddled with little worms—after we had eaten considerable quantities! There was another occasion when Ma Why asked if she could say a wee word at one meal time. Then she testified to the fact that the previous evening she hadn't been able to find us anything much to eat, but had discovered hidden away somewhere in a cupboard a very old can of fish. She had opened this tin, and having nothing else, she prayed over it and gave it to us, trusting we wouldn't suffer. Since none had been ill, she felt she ought to testify that the Lord had answered prayer! Needless to say, we used to pull her leg about it subsequently because, whenever we had fish, we would ask her if she had prayed over it."

6

FOUNDATION PRINCIPLES

As the C.L.C. Staff took shape, with the Adamses, Whybrows, Booths, Charlton Smiths, Fittons, and others, a conference was held with some of the W.E.C. leaders. The aim of this group was to bring clearly into focus the reasons for the existence of the C.L.C. (the Evangelical Publishing House as it was then called), the clarification of its objectives, its basic principles, and its relationship to W.E.C. It was this conference, held in Colchester, which gave official status to the C.L.C.

The most important act of recognition and affirmation was that, though C.L.C. had come into being as part of W.E.C. it was an autonomous Crusade within a Crusade. Its outreach would necessarily be wider than W.E.C. and its activities different. W.E.C. is a mission to the unevangelized, while C.L.C. was to be a literature ministry to all countries and all peoples, Christian and non-Christian, in home and foreign fields. It was to be a servant to all churches and organizations concerned with spreading the Gospel through literature. Decisions then made in seed form have been clarified and established through the years, so that what started as a Crusade within a Crusade is now better described as two Crusades side by side. How wisely guided we then were to emphasize the autonomy of this young group, inexperienced though they were, and to cast them from the beginning upon God. The years have justified it. That has not meant separation from W.E.C. But it has meant that while C.L.C. in its earlier years has been able to found itself on the spiritual principles upon which W.E.C. operates, and benefit by sharing in the material advantages of a mission with established headquarters, yet at the same time it has built firmly on its own foundations as a Literature Crusade and forged its own literacy links worldwide.

This should be made clear because, in reading its earlier history the readers will naturally notice how intertwined the C.L.C. has been with W.E.C., and may miss the important significance of this rightful distinction. W.E.C.– C.L.C. bonds have remained unbroken, though sometimes subjected to strains which in the end have only strengthened them. But they are mainly the bonds of spiritual fellowship with a certain amount of practical cooperation. For all their literature activities, opening of new fields, handling of finances, and all that comprises their literature ministry worldwide, C.L.C. runs its own affairs with its own workers' committees. They can therefore present themselves anywhere and to anyone as an autonomous mission. But in the main base headquarters, such as in Britain, U.S.A. and Australia, and on some fields where it is convenient, there is much intermingling of the workers. The candidates for both go through part of their testing period together; and the quarterly and annual staff meetings, where candidates are accepted and the work of the Crusades reviewed in general, are attended by both. Close links have also been maintained by the number of W.E.C. workers who have, with hearty approval, entered the C.L.C. ranks and vice versa. On all public platforms, in the homes of the friends of the Crusade and in the Prayer Batteries, the workers of the two Crusades are as one.

It should therefore be made clear that if at any time God should show it to be His will that C.L.C. should become completely independent of W.E.C., the C.L.C. of today could go right on as it is. It has been the privilege of the W.E.C. to "mother" this literature work in early days, but the era of leading strings is long over. C.L.C. in this its twenty-first year is C.L.C., as much as W.E.C. is W.E.C. in its fiftieth year.

Principles on which the C.L.C. was founded were, as in the W.E.C., sacrifice, faith and fellowship. A fourth principle is holiness. This is the standard for the churches God uses W.E.C. to found in the countries to which they go. That principle in C.L.C., where the objective is literature distribution and not church founding, is interpreted through its emphasis on, and handling of, the "deeper life" type of literature. The Crusade is also determined to be a spiritual ministry and not a business. Before all things, its objective is to bring people to a saving knowledge of Christ and to build up believers, literature being the means to that end. Not big business, but the bigness of Christ as man's All in all, Saviour, Lord, Life for time and eternity, is the sole interest, theme, reason for existence, objective in testimony of every activity of C.L.C.

Sacrifice as a principle means that those who join C.L.C. have a call from God (commissioned by God, not employed by man), and that therefore they are totally expendable in their calling: going anywhere, doing anything, living anyhow, prisoners of the Lord, bondslaves of Jesus Christ. The reward of bringing Christ to men and men to Christ far outweighs the cost.

Faith as a principle means first getting guidance from God in all plans of advance and expansion; then by the prayer of faith and word of faith ("when ye pray, believe that ye receive, and ye shall have," Mark 11:24), calling the things that be not as though they were; and finally proceeding with the plan of action on the basis that the needed supplies are on the way. Each worker joining the C.L.C. at home or abroad, equally lives individually by faith. It was agreed that profits from the sale of literature would be used for the maintenance and expansion of the work as the Lord would indicate. For personal needs each worker would depend directly upon God. We recognized that this, in a special way, meant that C.L.C. workers would be out on the deep with God. This is because, when workers live by faith in the evangelistic field, people know that they have no natural sources of supply; but when workers are a part of a literature mission, many will take it for granted and think it normal and right, that they should live on the profits of their sales. But the dangers of human security and mechanical supply sapping the life of total dependence upon God, in a work which necessarily has to be run on regular business lines, confirmed us in maintaining the faith principle for each worker in the face of a charge of foolishness and fanaticism. Twenty-one years have confirmed in general that we were rightly guided. Tests in individual lives have been many and sometimes fierce. Humanly speaking, it is no light thing to see God supplying the daily bread and family needs of workers who spend all their hours packing books, behind the counter in a store, or at an office desk, and who seldom go out to meetings and fellowships which bring them and their ministry more into the public eye. When the C.L.C. began to open work on foreign fields, it was decided that there would be a gift fund apart from literature profits, and what came into that fund should be divided among the field workers. This method of field supply has remained unchanged. However, a few years ago it was also decided that C.L.C. fields should include the home bases, which are not just sending bases for foreign lands, but also have their own literature ministry. Therefore, home base workers now receive a small monthly percentage of what comes into the gift fund.

But as we view the rapid worldwide expansion of C.L.C., the number of workers who have joined, and the recruits coming forward to a type of work which has not the glamour of a pioneer mission field, we are as sure as ever that the founding and maintaining of C.L.C. on the faith basis has been sealed by God in the twenty-one years of material supplies without appeal to man. It has also been instrumental in maintaining C.L.C.—an efficient business and yet not a business—on the tight rope walk of an agency of a supernatural God, in a world which is only too prone to drag down on to a material level even the agencies of God.

The third principle, fellowship, has had importance in the development of the C.L.C., because it has safeguarded the Crusade from the separation between controllers and controlled, which so easily becomes entrenched in a Christian society—the executive board in one group, the missionaries in another. But C.L.C. believes that the voice of the Spirit, as in a local church in the New Testament, is heard through the members of the whole church or society, and not through a selected few in authority. Therefore, the workers themselves should be their own executive authority, which also means that the workers recognize themselves to be the work and not merely employed in it. They thus become fused into it and into the fellowship as being themselves the fellowship. When those who make decisions are the ones to carry them out, they are likely to be more cautious in what they decide. This also has been amply proven through the years. The management in all home bases and fields is the whole staff of workers although smaller committees make day to day decisions for which they are responsible to their staff and to the Annual Conference.

Decisions by a large staff are arrived at more slowly. Sometimes the method may even seem tedious. Not all speak up, and the thought arises: what's the use of silent members? But, silent or vocal, it means that all feel a part, and decisions reached through patiently awaiting the revelation of the mind of God to all, have the strength of the whole group pulling at their oars in unison. One other helpful consequence is that differences, which often arise and are meant to arise because of the variety among the members of the body, and undercurrents which flow as a result, can be brought to the surface and channelled back into the main stream by the principles of patient open fellowship.

With principles go business methods. It must by no means be thought, because pioneering days were rough and ready, and the work appeared almost fantastically flimsy, that this is how a C.L.C. can be developed. No. If God calls a Christian business into being, it is to His glory that it is run as a first-class business. Ken Adams and those with him have worked on that basis from the beginning. In the various departments they are constantly aiming at improving the standards of stocks, bookkeeping, business deals with publishers, the bookstores, window dressing, the book displays on the shelves, courtesy to customers, efficient packing and prompt delivery of mail orders, the C.L.C. magazine *Floodtide,* the development of the foreign work, publishing and printing, art work and designing, auditing accounts, bills paid, etc. Mr. Whybrow with the accounts in those early days, Phil Booth with the foreign developments, Les Fitton with his outstanding gifts in the ordering and handling of stock, Dorrie Brooking in the bookstore with her long years of experience, Miriam Booth and Bonnie Hanson as editors of *Floodtide,* Eric Rodda in the Mail Order Department, and the many others who have joined through the years—each served without stint in their respective ministries. We shall hear more of the experience of some of these, but it was a miracle of God which welded into a working, efficient, spiritual team, a group of men and women who, with few exceptions, had had no previous experience of their jobs.

The objectives facing this fast growing Crusade were put into print following this first Workers' Conference in London in 1942. They have since been expanded and enlarged but it will be of interest, we believe, to quote from these original findings as embodied in a little booklet entitled *What is the E.P.H.?* (Later revised under the title *What is the C.L.C.?*) It does repeat a point or two already mentioned but the reader will note in subsequent chapters the central place these early principles and policies continue to have.

"The first objective is to open evangelical book centres in every city or town in the British Isles where needed, for the specific purpose of spreading evangelical literature over the widest possible area in the shortest possible time. Then, as other countries feel led to follow suit (U.S.A. and the Dominions, for example) to enlarge into an international C.L.C., including in due course branches in the more advanced mission fields where such book centres could be usefully opened.

"The next point made indubitably clear was that the shops are to confine their sales strictly to evangelical literature true to the Word of God, so that purchasers can feel quite sure that all they see and buy in our branches will build up readers in their most holy Faith, or point the unconverted to the Saviour.

"It was also resolved that the standards of the centres should be as high as possible so as to bring credit to the Lord when compared with the modern shops around, and yet of course without undue extravagance or worldly self-advertisement. The aim should be to make every shop really presentable in a simple way, so that it should not fail to recommend its priceless goods by a shoddy appearance, poorness of window display, or paucity of stock.

"The profoundly important principle was also decided upon that each book centre should be first and foremost a spiritual power house; that the workers should be out to win souls and help fellow-Christians by personal contacts, this being more important than the sale of books; that all the denominations and branches of Christ's Church in the town should be made to feel that the shop belonged to all, and was at their service; that the C.L.C. should minister to the unification of the Body of Christ in each place; and that the workers should be available to help the churches by speaking at meetings.

"One final point was stressed — to stimulate the publication of new books and encourage authors with a message. The C.L.C. has been founded as a publishing house as well as a selling agent, and it plans to constantly extend this branch of its activities."

7

ADVANCE INTO THE IMPOSSIBLE

C.L.C. as a literature mission started with two natural obstacles to progress. The first was the inexperience of the young staff, only one of them having any literary training; the second was the wholly inauspicious moment to begin a literature distribution ministry in wartime Britain. The opening of new shops was forbidden, the obtaining of supplies of books by a new organization in such a time of shortage highly unlikely. There was only one answer. If God was in it, the impossible would happen —and it did.

"The Lord had begun to bring others to us," says Ken Adams, "and by this time the vision had grown to the point that we were now going to have bookstores up and down the country. At this stage there were no indications as to just what God was going to do. Then things began to move. The war was on and we were to learn a few things about trying to develop a literature work in wartime. An article appeared in *World Conquest* (the W.E.C. magazine) stating that we were going to open two hundred bookstores—a somewhat rash statement (written by Norman Grubb!) as never in our wildest dreams did we ever mention two hundred bookstores. However, we were later to learn that there was something prophetic even in this apparently rash statement. The one thing undeniably clear at this time was that God had definitely spoken to us about opening Christian bookstores in needy cities throughout the country. No sooner had this article appeared than the *Daily Press* came out with some articles which said that the British Board of Trade was now clamping down on the opening of new stores, and in future no one could open any kind of shop without government permission. So here were the two articles; one in *World Conquest* written by Norman Grubb and the other in the British newspapers written by the powers that be. Who was right? Which one were we to follow? Here were two plain declarations of intention: One by a few simple followers of the Lord; the other by an influential government acting in the best interest of a country engaged in all-out war.

"Our answer was emphatic and uncompromising. The simple statement in *World Conquest* was not a rash presentation of man-made intention but the outlining of a program based upon the sure Word of the Lord to our hearts. This then we must follow. Now in effect we were saying, 'Mr. Government, you'll have to watch it happen. And what's more, you'll have to come to our aid and provide these permits!'

"There was a brother in the city of Leicester in the Midlands who, along with other friends, was becoming burdened about the soldiers in their city, who were mainly cadets, young men training as officers. This friend sent to W.E.C. Headquarters to buy some copies of a little gospel leaflet written by Bill Pethybridge entitled, *A New Life for You.* These came wrapped up in an old copy of *World Conquest.* This particular issue had the article in it (the first that ever appeared in print) about this vision of Christian bookstores up and down the country, and it caught his eye. 'That's the very thing we should be doing,' he said, and wrote a short note asking for details, to which I replied.

"Two months went by and then by a long-distance telephone call he said, 'I'm most interested. I've been looking for some property and have found a building that I think will be adequate. Could you come up immediately and look it over?' Well, I tell you! It isn't only people in America that move fast! This was really going some!

"The building was right on the corner in quite a strategic area. It was a fine store but had no fixtures in it, just the four walls. Behind were a couple of rooms and a kitchen, and upstairs several rooms that were most suitable for a soldiers' canteen. 'Why don't you folks take the ground floor with the bookstore and the rooms behind?' he suggested. 'If you supply the stock and run the bookstore we'll be responsible for running the soldiers' work. Perhaps the workers you send can help us with this. Let's try it for a year. If the idea doesn't work and the bookstore is not a success we can forget about it and I won't charge you any rent. If it succeeds we can talk about the future later.' That sounded like a pretty good proposition, so I went back to Colchester and presented the suggestion to our little group. By this time the Lord had sent us two more workers, Freda Prothero and Nora Miller. We all felt they would be the couple to send and began to make plans accordingly.

"But, to open up a store in Leicester, we now had to get a government permit. This was quite a battle. We prayed much as we submitted our application. Weeks later the phone rang and word came from the Board of Trade in Leicester that the permit had been granted. Our worker who answered it, Gwen Robinson, responded with 'Hallelujah' on the telephone. I don't know what the person thought at the other end! But with us there was great rejoicing.

"When Pa Why and I arrived at the shop, we called in a shopfitter and outlined to him what we needed. 'We shall want shelves along this wall, counters here, and shelving in the windows as well.' It was a big store with corner windows. The man had been making notes all along the way and as we finished, he looked at me and said,

" 'Mr. Adams, you *do* know there's a war on, don't you?'

" 'Yes,' I said, 'there is, but what's that got to do with it?'

" 'Well,' he replied, 'we are not now able to get all the supplies needed and you've ordered a tremendous amount of wood here. I don't believe we can get a quarter of it. But I'll apply for it anyway.'

" 'You go right ahead,' I suggested. 'You apply for it and we'll pray for it.'

" 'I believe God too,' he said, 'but I don't know that God can supply wood for shelving.'

"Two weeks later I was up there again, this time to stay and help get things actually established. The two workers went up with me as well. When we walked into the store we were a little disappointed to see that the shelves weren't up, but there in the middle of the floor was the wood piled high. I turned to our workers and said, 'Looks like prayer has done something around here anyway!' A little later the shopfitter came in and looked at me with a grin on his face and said, 'Mr. Adams, I don't understand it yet. I had seven or eight other jobs in hand needing wood, so I included these when submitting your application. One job was for some English oak in a nearby church. Believe it or not, the job for the English oak was turned down and this wood, every stick of which is imported, was granted!' I suppose to his dying day, that man will never forget the testimony he himself witnessed to a God Who can provide adequate shelving in wartime."

As we have mentioned previously, the move into the Leicester store constituted our first expansion from Colchester. One of the two pioneer workers who opened this center is now with the Lord—Freda Prothero. What a go-getter for God she was! Things hummed when she was around with her devoted co-worker, Nora Miller, in the bookstore or at endless meetings. She was a magnet that drew young people to Christ.

"We went on from there to other cities," continues Ken. "Altogether six stores needed permits during those war years, including the big London store. I will only tell of one other—the store in Stockport on the outskirts of Manchester. Getting this permit took a long time. We were turned down three times, but we battled through and would not take 'no' for an answer, until they finally gave us a 'yes.' By this time things were getting more and more difficult.

"It was the same old story. We called in a shopfitter and outlined to him our needs. This man was less polite and said, 'Don't you know there's a war on? You're just talking ridiculous. I'll tell you what. You get the wood and I'll do the work. Let's put it that way,' and with that he left.

" 'All right,' I said, 'we'll call you back later.' When I returned that night to the home where I was staying, my host said, 'Look at this!' and showed me the newspaper of the previous day. Now why would you read yesterday's paper today unless there is a guiding of the Lord in it? In this paper was an advertisement saying that in a few days' time there would be an auction sale of shelving, fixtures, fittings, glass-top counters, etc. We discovered later that this equipment belonged to a candy firm, and because of the shortage of candy they had been forced to close down many of their shops. They had stored all the fixtures and fittings in a big warehouse, hoping for the day when they could start up again. The government came along (it's amazing how the government worked for us) and commandeered the warehouse so the firm had no alternative but to get rid of all their fixtures and fittings. Again we found ourselves at an auction sale. Once more our heads nodded, and soon we had purchased an ample supply of shelving and counters. We got it back to the store, and then went around to the shopfitter and said, "When can you start?'

" 'Start what?' he asked.

" 'Start putting up the shelves in our bookstore as you said you would.' You can imagine the look on that fellow's face when he walked into the store the next day.

" 'Where in the world . . . ?' he exclaimed.

" 'It's in the world all right,' I said, 'It's right here in the store.' So once again, we had witnessed a miracle of God, and each store has had a story in itself along this same line.

"Then there was the actual stocking of the stores. It was all very well to say we were going to open bookstores, but where would we get sufficient stock? In this also we were to see the miracles of God over and over again. Conditions were such that when you would write to a Bible publisher and order a gross of their cheapest Bible, ten would arrive! You would be politely informed, 'This is your quota for the next three months!' And here we were blithely planning to open new stores!

"But these were problems with which we did not need to concern ourselves. The Lord had assured us that He would handle the matter as each new need arose. And so He did. We had seen it as *His* provision when our first requests for stock had been met with such generous coöperation. Now as the work expanded this same kindly attitude was maintained. There was always a ready desire to help: I have a suspicion that some were frankly intrigued by our very audacity! Be that as it may, the fact remains for the record, these business men almost without exception stood by us in our need. We will be eternally grateful for their help—and their patience. With the rapid development of the program we sometimes ran a bit behind with our payments and this would call for some friendly consultation. In due course, and with the Lord's blessing on the sales, we would catch up and all would be well."

Leslie Fitton joined the C.L.C. in those early days and for the seventeen years he was with the Crusade, both in Britain and in the U.S.A., he was God's gift to us in the book ordering and stock department. He was particularly concerned with the problem of stock when the time came for opening the main C.L.C. store in London. "One of the many problems confronting the opening of a large London store was the provision of many thousands of books and Bibles for an initial stock," Leslie writes. "At this time there were very few evangelical books in print, and since there was an acute paper shortage, editions were very small and usually were reported out of print after only a few weeks or months. Therefore we decided to 'stock-pile' supplies for about a year in advance of the opening of the London store. These supplies, together with others made possible by coöperative publishers at the time the store opened, ensured an adequate supply of many titles. However, there was still the serious problem of having even a reasonable supply of Bibles on hand, and it was decided that we should approach one of the four Bible publishers with a definite request for five thousand Bibles.

"An interview was arranged with a director of this company—a man who was very well known throughout the British book trade. He proved to be extremely interested in the C.L.C. story, especially when he heard that C. T. Studd, founder of the W.E.C., was a brother of Sir Kynaston Studd, a former Lord Mayor of London, with whom he had been very friendly. However, he pointed out that the largest quota of Bibles, of the type we were asking, was two hundred copies, and this quantity was only allowed to a large organization. There was also the question of our financial status! 'Do we need faith for the payment, even if such a fantastic request could be granted?' he asked. We assured him that this would not be necessary! Amazingly enough, we were told a few days later that five thousand Bibles would be made available to us almost immediately, with the added admonition, 'Don't put too many on show at once, or we'll be in trouble!' This was indeed the Lord's doing, and marvelous in our eyes."

"So often we have said that C.L.C. was not a business, but a ministry," adds Ken Adams. "And yet the very fact that it has this big business element in it has puzzled many. They just don't understand it. But praise the Lord, He has led us on step by step over the years, only to witness the same sort of miracle over and over again.

"We now have eleven bookstores in the British Isles. Although we laughed at Norman Grubb and chided him for his article on the two hundred bookstores, God actually brought something similar into the visible, though in a different way. With the stock situation steadily improving we were able to share supplies with other struggling bookstores which were just on the verge of closing down because they were unable to get adequate stock. To this day, there are stores in Britain which look to C.L.C. as the one that came to their rescue in their time of dire need. Over the years, we have served well over three hundred British bookstores with our Christian literature program. It has changed a bit during the past few years. At one time we had quite an extensive wholesale department, but as the war finished and publishers were able to get back into the field of publishing, there was less and less need for us to do it. Also, our own worldwide program was growing so rapidly that we had to drop some of the service to these national bookstores and concentrate more on the overseas work. But this somewhat anticipates the next chapter—the move from Colchester to London."

8

THE SEVEN-STORIED MIRACLE

From quite early days Ken Adams talked about the necessity of moving C.L.C. Headquarters and central bookstore to London. Although we could see the sense of this, we did not encourage Ken, for several things made it seem nonsense to many of us. It appeared absurd to think of such a move in war days. It would entail tremendous added expense in overheads. Moreover, there was only a small team of workers, and the business itself was surely too limited for occupation of a large set of offices and a city shop. But he stuck to his point, returned to it again and again, and finally began to take action—against our advice.

"A word that has become very precious to us as we have widened out over the years," says Ken, is in Esther 4. We remember Mordecai's deep concern because of the dire need of his people, the Jews. Then came the clear revelation from the Lord and the word of inspiration that the Queen could provide a solution. He twice repeated his appeal to her, and put the penetrating question, 'Who knoweth whether thou art come to the kingdom for such a time as this? The Queen's carefully weighed response indicated her complete committal to a noble cause—'I will go and see the King . . . and if I perish, I perish.' For us that has been a key note down the years— the thought that we believe God brought C.L.C. into the picture, and gave us vision and burden for such a time as this. This conviction has continually deepened, particularly these last ten years, with the great thrust of communism and the great literacy campaigns producing eighty million new literates each year. It has led to a readiness on our part, as with Queen Esther, to pay any price to fulfill our commission. We are still only just scratching the surface but, praise the Lord, we are in being and are moving ahead bit by bit."

The move to London at that time did seem to many of us an "if I perish, I perish" situation! Ken can best tell the story himself. "The Ludgate Hill move was one of the major advances of the work, and it was an advance that came about directly as a result of the growing vision and commission God had given us. We were beginning to see some of the possibilities in an overseas ministry and were saying, 'If we're going to put this thing through and see God develop a worldwide literature ministry, we'll have to do this from London.' London is literally the heart of the British Isles, and every major industry has its head-quarters there. By and large the publishing world is in London; so we began to see that if we were really going to get to grips with this vision we would have to move to the City. As is often the case, you don't get a complete picture all at once; the Lord begins to drop seed thoughts along the way, and this was a seed thought. We often talked casually among ourselves, 'You know, one day maybe we'll have to move to London.'

"I happened to be in the City on one occasion, doing some book buying, and was walking up Ludgate Hill. I noticed some empty buildings on which was a sign board indicating the name and address of the real estate office, and the thought came to me: it wouldn't be a bad idea to find out how much it's going to cost to come up to London. So right there on the spot I took down the name and address of the agent.

"Next day I shared this with Pa Why, and sent the agent a brief letter. The reply was quite encouraging. The building was No. 37 Ludgate Hill, so Pa Why and I went up to look it over. It was a five-storied building, with a very nice window and display showroom. It was leased by a duplicating firm. But strangely enough, as we looked it over and liked it, we said, 'This won't do, it's not large enough!' But we noticed next door, No. 39, which looked like a good building too. Many windows had been blown out and so were boarded up; but we peeped through and saw it was quite a sizeable showroom, with an opening in the ceiling and what looked like a second showroom upstairs. We found that the rent of No. 37 was reasonable and we thought: that's not too bad for the City of London. We had really expected more, though from our £52 a year in Colchester it was quite a leap! Anyhow we decided to look at No. 39. It was thick with dust, not only because it had stood empty, but also had been well shaken by the bombs, which had been plentiful in that area around St. Paul's Cathedral. The building had a basement and six floors. For years it had been a china and glassware store. I could remember it quite well from the many times I had passed it on my first job in London. 'Well,' we said, 'it's got possibilities.' But the thing that intrigued us was the reasonable rent of this building. 'This *has* got possibilities!' we said.

"We obtained an 'order to view' from the agents who were acting for the landlords in respect of this property. The condition of the interior was awful, equaling that of the exterior; it was all very depressing. A subsequent interview with the Chief Surveyor to the City of London relevant to our renting the premises wasn't very encouraging either. However, the Lord witnessed to our hearts that this was to be the place, so we decided to push at all possible 'doors' trusting the Lord to check us somewhere if we were on the wrong track. So negotiations were commenced with the landlords for a lease on 39 Ludgate Hill.

"We knew a keen Christian man, one of the partners in a firm of Surveyors and Estate Agents in the City, and requested him to come and look this place over. He came, made his inspection, shook his head, saying, 'Mr. Adams, I would advise you to leave it alone. This is an old building. The necessary alterations and renovations will be very costly. Besides, who can say what the situation will be like on "The Hill" before the war ends, or after for that matter.' But we had commenced negotiations; the war was not over, and although we did not know it, the attack on London by rockets and pilotless planes was yet to come.

"Then all unexpectedly it happened. Out of the blue, as it were, came the information from the landlords to the effect that owing to a technical point outside the control of either party, the whole matter must be left in abeyance indefinitely. Naturally, we were greatly disappointed, but we were to prove that God was indeed working out His purposes in the situation. No further investigations were made concerning any other properties. We knew He would take us to London in His own time and way.

"Then one day a letter came—from the landlords of 39 Ludgate Hill! It was just a brief note which said: 'Nearly a year ago you were interested in a property in London, and we are wondering whether you are still interested.' We looked at this letter and said, 'Bless me, here it is!' It didn't take us long to decide. We wrote back a six-line letter saying we were still interested in the property, but only on the same terms as previously presented. Two weeks went by, then came another letter: 'We are interested in your proposition and will be glad to talk further with you.'

"We went up to see our real estate friend again. He said, 'Mr. Adams, I can hardly believe this. I just don't understand it. It looks as though God has certainly been leading you.' So he arranged for a surveyor who went from top to bottom of this seven-storied building, outside as well as inside, and itemized 365 repair jobs that needed to be done—one for every day in the year! This we submitted through him to the landlords, stating that we were prepared to sign a contract for a fourteen-year lease, providing they would insert a clause covering an important technicality and undertake to renovate the entire building according to the surveyor's appraisal. The next thing we expected was a letter saying that some of these repairs were not necessary, and 'here is our list of the jobs we are willing to do.' No such letter came. The next communication was: 'Here is the contract. You sign it and we will do all the 365 jobs in the building'; and sure enough they did. Because of the wartime shortage of material there were a few they couldn't complete at the time, such as the elevator; but because of this they reduced the rent until the elevator was put in working order some years later. When our surveyor heard that, he said, 'Mr. Adams, this is too good to be true. I just can't believe it but, praise the Lord, I'm rejoicing with you.'

"What a thrill it was to see it all coming into the visible. When it was completed many passers-by commented that it was the brightest and most attractive building in all the City of London. With so little repair work going on in Britain immediately following the war this newly decorated building certainly did stand out. To us it was a silent but conspicuous testimony to the faithfulness of our miracle-working God."

But it must be admitted, however, that there had been misgivings in the hearts of some as to the wisdom of such a sizeable undertaking. And now, before the actual signing of the contract, agreement had to be reached by the Board of Trustees. These men had been quietly watching and, as the clear evidences of this proposition being of the Lord unfolded, they readily gave their consent—though in one sense, doing so, was tantamount to a personal leap of faith.

"I remember so clearly," recalls Ken, 'the day we took Norman Grubb with us for a final look over the building.

When the inspection was ended, we went across the road for a stimulating cup of tea in the A. B. C. Restaurant. There we sat looking across to 39 Ludgate Hill, Rubi with a long, serious face, hoping he wasn't being tricked into something. Finally he said, 'If you and Pa Why and the rest in C.L.C. feel satisfied, I'll go along with you. But to me it seems far too big, and it will be a tremendous financial undertaking.'

" 'Rubi,' I said, 'if we mean what we say, if we mean that we are going to reach around the world with literature, it's not only not too big, it will soon be too small.' Secretly he thought: That's Ken, with one of his rather wild statements!'

"Not more than two years later we were seriously talking about the need for more room because we just didn't know where to put everything! Less than ten years later, we had acquired a second building in London as a warehouse to stock the books which we were now buying in much larger quantities, and also for a print shop. So, to the glory of God, we have seen the seal of His approval on some of these wild schemes and adventures out into the unknown."

9

THIS IS THE HOUSE OF GOD

With the main C.L.C. team moving to London—the hub of the British world of Christian literature, publishers and bookstores—C.L.C. would no longer be a provincial backstreet bookroom. Under the shadow of St. Paul's Cathedral, all passers-by would be looking into their display windows. Would these attract the attention of prospective buyers? Many customers would be sampling the range of books for sale within, browsing around if they found the atmosphere congenial, asking questions, making purchases. What standard of service would they find, and would the sales-workers be sensitive to human and spiritual need as well as to book selling? Would stocks in its two showrooms be well laid out, and the shop give the appearance of an up-to-date, wide-awake sales center? Salesmen would be paying visits from the different Christian publishers. Would they get the impression of a forward-moving organization, worth their special attention? Would the Mail Order Department have a good testimony to Christian efficiency by prompt dispatch and safe packing? Would accounts be paid on time and a good name ensured with creditors?

Mrs. Doris (Dorrie) Brooking, with her previous long experience in a Christian bookstore and her ever sensitive concern for the spiritual needs of customers, was the first of God's gifts to the Sales Department. She had joined the C.L.C. in Colchester, but now, on arrival at Ludgate Hill, she took full charge of the two sales floors as well as training many newcomers in book selling both as a business and a ministry.

"My first few years in C.L.C. were spent in Colchester," she writes. "C.L.C. was then in its precarious infancy. Ken and Bess, and Ma and Pa Why, gave us our duties in the home and in the shop. What a worker Ken was, setting us an excellent example. Despite the war and the frequently disturbed nights during the blitz, when the bombers came overhead in relays, we got through a lot of work, reading, praying and planning. One feature of the work in those early days was the Saturday night 'squash' for soldiers. These were evenings of great joy, first 'fishing' the men and boys in, and then packing them into the shabby lounge. Years later, when I was serving in the C.L.C. London shop, a well-dressed business man said to me, 'Weren't you one of the "oldish ladies" at Colchester, who ran the "squashes" for soldiers? I'm "Nobby" Clark. Although I've been saved several years, I shall never forget the night God found me, and I came to Jesus, along with others, after a "squash" meeting. We were all kneeling on the floor, and you three ladies helped us.' Such facts could be repeated. It is thrilling to recall them! There was the lady doctor who sought and found Jesus the Saviour. She came to know Him as the Burden-bearer. Her burdens were great—a broken marriage and a breaking heart. Never shall I forget her, as we prayed together in that little room. In faltering accents she prayed; 'Lord Jesus, I come. Oh, what love, how can I thank Thee.' Personal inward battles there were, but in the light of souls finding peace with God, they melted away.

"From 1946 the work of C.L.C. began to open out to a wider and indeed worldwide field. We moved into 39 Ludgate Hill, to forward and establish the work of distribution. With eager interest we watched the progress of the shop-fitters as we attended to incoming stock — surrounded on all sides by piles of parcels. At last the ground floor was ready, though not completed. We got

busy with the window display and shop's layout. Then
with thanksgiving to God, one golden summer day in
July 1946, we opened the shop and so started the Retail
Department of C.L.C. London. At the simple dedication
service many friends joined us in praise and thanksgiving
to God.

"There were just two of us to whom Ken passed on
the responsibility of the Retail Department in those early
London days. He said to us, 'If you take in so much each
week, the profits will be sufficient to pay the rent of the
building, then the profits from the mail order work can
be used for advance.' We gladly accepted the challenge.
We worked and prayed. At first it was uphill work; we
seemed to be tugging but getting nowhere! Then, sure
enough, we were getting under way. Soon we were moving
steadily towards our goal. We doubled our activity, and
slowly, in small increases, the sales came. In less than six
months we had well passed our goal. New workers joined
us, and we were now able to take on the responsibility
of another sales floor. We formed what became known as
the 'Retail Prayer Meeting.' We made a list of needs for
development and saw God work. We prayed for £100
for inside fittings. A personal friend sent me this exact
amount for the work. She had no idea at all we were
praying for that sum! But when with enthusiasm I took
it to Ken and Pa, they said, 'Perhaps your friend has sent
it for literature, not for dead shelves!' My heart sank, but
I wrote my friend telling her simply the facts, the need,
and our prayer. She replied expressing her desire that the
money be used for fittings." And Dorrie adds, "I think,
Ken, I was rather dogmatic in that situation. Please forgive me! The passing of the years has taken away a great
deal of the cocksure attitude that was mine in the earlier
days.

"Four of us drew up a few questions," she continues,
"to ask ourselves concerning our efficiency in serving
customers, our coping with daily routine and, above all,

our preparedness for spiritual contacts. They were these: Is my service to the customers, in obedience to the Lord who called me to serve them, defective? Then let me kindle my love by communion with the Lord. Is my confidence, compassion, human understanding and kindliness, feeble? Then let me have deeper communion by deliberate obedience. A Christian Literature Crusader who abides in Christ and Christ in him, exerts an influence among his customers and publishers' representatives that nothing can efface. Such a Crusader becomes a channel through whom the love of God flows in whatever he does.

"These are the questions I have had to answer over the years. Because in the two major responsibilities that have fallen to me—that of selling, and now of buying—I have encountered and had to deal with the problems resulting from sin, sorrow, anguish, heartache, misery, and sometimes unspeakable grief. We have had to be equipped for the task of selecting books true to the Scriptures in order that the Holy Spirit can use them to convict and wound, bind up and heal, enlighten and deliver. Unless the books bring the readers to Christ, we have accomplished little. In our London and branch shops we are continually busy with personal talks and prayer with people who are seeking spiritual help. Said a gentlemen in the London shop one day to the one who was serving him with books to meet a special need, 'All the heart specialists do not live on Harley Street!'

"There is much to encourage. We have seen many lives changed. We touch all types of people: Christians defeated by sin and longing for deliverance; Christians seeking a deeper life in the Holy Spirit; people in spiritual distress; people with inner conflicts; backsliders; the bereaved; folk who are hopeless and ill; people with stigma and tragedy in their lives; people who try to start arguments! Said a young lady to me, 'I want a holy book, written by the saints.' This lady, so attractive, so nicely dressed and with a foreign accent, walked with me to the bookshelves. Praying quietly, 'Lord, direct and choose through me,' I took from the shelves a copy of *The Hymns of Terstegen and Suso*. Said the lady before I could serve her further, 'This place feels holy. What is this place? The atmosphere here is more holy than St. Paul's. Who are you? Where am I?'

"You are in God's house, God is here and I am His servant. This is Literature House where every floor is dedicated to God for the distribution of holy books' (using her own term). She bought the book. She was a Roman Catholic seeking God. We have never seen her since.

"A lady about middle age entered the shop, restless, nervous, obviously ill and in need. She asked for an interesting book, 'One that will grip.' While being served, she said with disgust, 'Religion! Are all these books religious? I don't want religious stuff. I'm ill and bordering on a nervous breakdown. My life is in a mess. I cannot sleep. I must drown myself in something arresting — Sherlock Holmes, Agatha Christie or the like!'

" 'I, too, have been ill,' came the answer, 'and have known sorrow and grief. I, too, have read Sherlock Holmes, but he didn't help!'

" 'Oh, did any special author help you,' asked the customer.

"Taking up the Gospel of John in magazine format, I said, 'Jesus helped me. If you are heavy laden, He is the Burden-bearer. If you have sorrow, He will give you joy. If you are in darkness, He is the Light of the world. If you have sinned, God will forgive you because Jesus died.'

" 'Jesus! how can Jesus help me?' questioned the customer further.

" 'Jesus bore our sins and griefs and carried our sorrows. You can have peace now through the blood of His cross.'

"She was arrested by the Name of Jesus. She became

quieter. We walked to the shop door together. She left with the Gospel and a copy of a small booklet, *A New Life*. In less than ten minutes she was back again. Handing in a bunch of lovely flowers, she said, 'No one has ever spoken to me of Jesus before. No one has ever shown me understanding and kindness!' In a minute she was gone. We have never seen her again.

"Are we discouraged when we only touch the surface of such deep human need? No, we believe in the power of the Name of Jesus, in the power of the Blood of Jesus, in the power of the Word of God, in the power of the printed page, and last (but by no means least) we believe in the power of the love of God shed abroad in our hearts —and believing we rejoice.

"Another special feature of the work is giving guidance and direction to Christian workers in the choice of books. Pastors of churches; leaders of prayer groups; Bible study groups; Christian unions; superintendents and teachers of Sunday Schools; people in charge of bookstalls; evangelistic campaigns and young people's camps; all come to us for help. We also serve the personal workers, such as the little old-age pensioner who comes regularly once a month saying, 'I want me tracts to give out down our way,' or the titled lady who purchases from among the choicest publications to send to missionaries in India.

"Beside all this, there are the daily business matters connected with the work. In all the varied ministries we need to walk in simple dependence upon our Heavenly Father, seeking wisdom, guidance and strength for the daily task. There is no life so rich or so full of joy as that of serving people at the point of their greatest need."

10

DOWN TO EARTH IN A LITERATURE CRUSADE

"It is easy in Christian service to mistake the spectacular for the real," says Dorrie Brooking. "It is so easy to imagine that I would be a willing servant of Jesus Christ in terms of the glamorous (the pioneer missionary tramping through the forests), or in the public eye (name and fame), or in a ministry to hungry souls (being appreciated), or at least in having the satisfaction and variety of interest which comes from meeting people." But many jobs in C.L.C. are of an opposite nature—hidden, monotonous at a lonely desk, rarely meeting outsiders, physically and mentally demanding—and none more so than in the Packing Department.

To the drab basement of the London store God called a man, a glimpse into whose experiences represents those of the many others who have worked there through the years.

"There was nothing spectacular about my first contacts with C.L.C.," says Eric Rodda. "In fact they were so ordinary as to be wearisome to any reader, but God was in the seemingly ordinary."

Friends of Eric manned the C.L.C. bookshop in Chatham. Through frequent visits to the shop while he was still in the Army, and broad hints dropped regarding the need of workers, Eric began to realize that "they were trying to get me onto the fly paper." And they succeeded, or rather God through them, and after "many inner battles, unwillingness to step out, fears of what lay

This selection of productions from the Crusade press in the Philippines symbolizes the purpose of this worldwide literature ministry.

Above: The narrow picturesque street leading to the location where the C.L.C. vision and ministry was born.

Right: The early 18th Century building where C. H. Spurgeon once roomed and where C.L.C. began.

The first C.L.C. bookstore in Colchester, England.

The 1948 Conference in London where decisions regarding North American expansion were finalized.

The 1961 International Conference where there were representatives from the Philippines, Indonesia, South America, West Indies, North America, Europe and Great Britain.

Chatham—one of the stores for which a
permit was needed.

Literature House, 39 Ludgate Hill, London, England.

Browsing in one of the two well-stocked showrooms in
the London bookstore.

Committees handle Crusade affairs, national and worldwide.

The first Crusade print shop in London.

Stock moves out from the basement at Ludgate Hill.

Processing orders in the North American stockroom, Fort Washington, Pennsylvania.

Art, designing, editing and journalism are all a part of the Christian literature program.

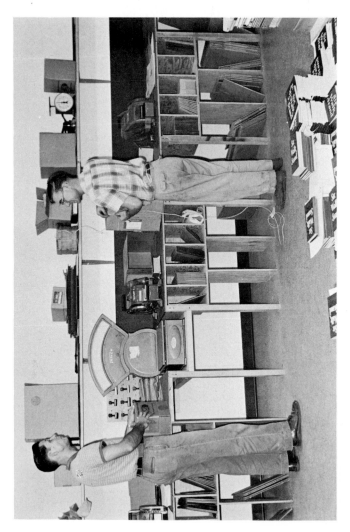

Books go to all parts of the world from the shipping room in Fort Washington.

Naka-san used this unique mode of literature evangelism
in Sapporo, Hokkaido, Japan.

A mobile bookshop in action in Jamaica, West Indies.

The window-witness in Hamburg, Germany.

Don Teall operates the Book Booth at the
Florence Trade Exhibition, Italy—1961.

The C.L.C. bookcenter in Rennes, France.

Front view of the C.L.C. North American administration building, Fort Washington, Pennsylvania.

ahead, and difficult home circumstances," Eric stepped
out. His first "happy six months" were at Chatham, with
the thrill of "actually working in a bookshop, contacting
people, making new friends, and enjoying the practical
side of things such as rearranging the shop shelving."

Then came the inevitable move to London. "The
General Secretary," recounts Eric, "invited me to come
up for a time to see if the Lord had indeed called me
into the C.L.C. fellowship. I came up to Ludgate Hill
in March 1948 and have been here ever since! Then
came my introduction to the basement. My first impression was anything but favorable—two large, ugly under-
ground rooms, the inner one in use as the Mail Order Department where the orders were serviced and dispatched.
Huge shelves lined the walls. These were once used as
storage space for china articles; unfortunately for us they
had been recently whitewashed, so that every time we
rubbed against them we looked as if we were painters
and decorators instead of book packers. The place was
truly uninviting; but I was eager to get the books out,
and, after all, this was not to be my permanent scene of
operation! Little did I know what the Lord had in store
for me."

A brief outline by Eric of the behind-the-scene activities
of a mail order department will not be too technical to
give us an insight into a literature missionary in action.
"The only other person in the basement when I started
to work there was a candidate for overseas. Leslie Fitton
was in charge of the Mail Order Department, and with
him I had much happy fellowship in the work. This
small team was joined later by two others. In those early
days we serviced each of our seven branch shops with all
their requirements. Usually Leslie dealt with the branch
orders, charging around the warehouse at high speed and
quickly writing the titles and quantities on an invoice.
Later as I became familiar with the stock and the location
of the different titles, I helped in this task. It was back

in those days also that what we called our 'District Representative' scheme was born. Some interested friends began to ask how they could help in the spread of Christian literature. From a very small beginning that side of the work has grown tremendously, and today we have over 150 agents playing a vital part in the distribution of Christian literature throughout the British Isles.

"The volume of business to traders also increased, as in those days we offered attractive discounts on other publishers' books. Many small Bible depots bought supplies from us. But the increase was not only evident in the home trade. Many who had bookshops overseas also wrote to us for supplies; and through this channel we were able to send books to almost every country where English is spoken, such as South Africa, India, Ceylon, Australia and New Zealand. Another outlet for literature which gladdened our hearts was through missionaries serving with W.E.C. and with other Missions in lands where people could understand English. Over the years we have sent literature into approximately 125 such countries.

"Although I was involved up to the hilt in the work in those early days, yet I was not a candidate. I had not dutifully filled in the Mission application papers, nor acquiesced with *Principles and Practices!* The price seemed too great to me; I wanted my freedom. The message of the Cross Life, the laying down deliberately of my life for the sake of others, did not appeal to me. I recognized this to be of the flesh. I knew that in order to be a blessing to others I must first be identified with the Lord Jesus. 'The corn of wheat to multiply, must fall into the ground and die'—die, die to the self life. But how much of the self life there is to die! How much there was in me. Nevertheless I could not continue to hold back; I tried to back out, but the Holy Spirit was urging me to go forward. To join a Mission which offered no earthly security was asking a lot of one with little faith. Then I began to think: had I not trusted God with the most important thing of all, my eternal salvation? Could I not then trust this same God for the supply of my material needs? After much prayer I filled in those papers and with much trepidation handed them in. I did not want to join C.L.C., but God wanted me to and to have gone out of His will would have meant disaster.

"Years later God met with us as a mission through the ministry of Ivor Davies, who had seen and experienced revival in the Congo. Some of us, myself included, were hungry for God. We wanted God to do something among us, we did not know what; we just asked, and God came. Sins of the flesh were brought to the light. God met with me personally and I had to put certain matters right. Our God is holy. He cannot dwell with sin, so I had to be cleansed. So simple and yet so real was that experience, I shall be eternally grateful to God for it.

"Leslie Fitton had left us for the U. S. A. Headquarters in 1953, and the Lord called Dorrie Brooking into the Mail Order Department. I was sorry to see Leslie go; we had shared much together, and our fellowship had been happy. Now I was called to work together with Dorrie—a woman! My reaction was not favorable, in fact I wanted to go somewhere else; but again I proved that the Lord knew what He was doing, and we have had profitable times of fellowship together through the years which have followed. Differences there have been, but as we have looked to Him the differences have all been resolved.

"Over the years the Mail Order Department has changed greatly. At the beginning we operated in one large section of the basement; now the whole basement is used. The partitions have long since disappeared; we have even expanded into one of the upstairs floors, the whole of the second floor now being used by Mail Order. Our first big problem was when we saw the need to replan the basement and erect new shelving. Through

the increased volume of trade, more and more books had
to be stored somehow. We were able to buy steel shelving,
and at that time the Lord called William Sanderson, an
engineer, into our ranks, so we had a steel erector all
lined up for the big job. At the same time we were able
to cover with ceiling boards the huge beams which supported the floor above. The floor also received a new
look, with a plastic substance covering the bare concrete.
Then came fluorescent lighting, and new packing benches
which stretched in a continuous line along one side, so
that the packers earned the name of the 'Knights of the
long table.' How much the world owes to the men (and
occasionally women) who over the years have toiled day
in, day out, at that long table, packing parcels for so
many parts of the world, only eternity will reveal. Despite
all the increased space used, the work is growing to such
an extent that today we seek new and larger premises.*
Praise God for all these advances.

"The improvements have not been limited only to the
building itself. God has enabled us to devise better and
more efficient systems for the running of the whole department. Books have been classified, so orders can be
filled more quickly. Our 'to follow' system also has been
revolutionized. Now, if a book is out of stock at the time
of ordering, the system assures that the customer will
receive it as soon as it is again available. This has
progressed a long way from the days when 'to follows'
were sort of 'hit or miss.'

"The stock card system, first introduced by Leslie
Fitton, is still in use today. By this we can tell how
many copies of any particular title have been sold from
the time we first stocked it. These cards also tell us at
which time of the year a certain line sells, and so are an
invaluable guide to the one who buys the stock. As the
systems have improved, there has been, nevertheless, an

*Extra premises have now been obtained — See page 79

increasing need to rely on Him for daily wisdom, for enablement to give eye to detail, and for power to glorify Him in a backroom job.

"Interesting, too, has been the growth of our catalog since we opened Ludgate Hill in 1946. The first one produced contained sixteen pages, including two pages of Christmas cards and calendars. In 1961 we sent out a seventy-two page catalog, with a four-page folder of Christmas cards and calendars and an eight-page folder of sacred records. It is one of the most comprehensive catalogs of Bibles and Christian literature in Britain today.

"A list of new titles and reprints, called *Book News* is sent out periodically to our Book Agents and to many overseas centers. Another means of advertising we now use extensively is inserting leaflets about books in every parcel. Our ministry is the distribution of the Word of God and books that tell of Him. We in the Mail Order do not have the thrill of personal contacts, but we do reach souls because the literature we distribute is the fuel handled in our branch shops and by our Book Agents. These agents give of their spare time to operate book tables in their churches, do door-to-door visitation, or man a stall at a market. We also touch souls among our many retail customers who write to us for their book needs. We serve the world from Ludgate Hill; wherever a postal system operates we can send books.

"We have had many ups and downs. There are times when it has seemed as if we just could not get through our rush period prior to Christmas, but year by year He gives strength to the dedicated team—Dorrie Brooking, Allan Race, Phyllis Hall, Dorothy Raxworthy, Jack Dawney, Kay Taylor, Grace Rodda and myself, helped by others who come in temporarily just when we need them.

"To quote from *The Highway of Print:* 'This is not a human enterprise. It is of God, building a highway for the coming of the King, a highway over which the redeemed may walk, a highway of hearts made ready. The path of print may lead to that glorious highway, if we faithfully tend it and if we walk upon it in the very company of Christ Himself. He, the Incarnate Word, is the Highway, when our goal is God.' "

It was no light thing for a woman, Dorrie Brooking, to take the important, responsible position Leslie Fitton had held. "Something difficult, unwanted, had happened," she tells of that time, "and the staff were gathered in an upstairs room. Changes were taking place, and Leslie Fitton was shortly to leave us for the work in North America. Leslie was the buyer and business manager of C.L.C. London, yet it was only too true that he must go forward to take up the responsibility in the U. S. A. Loud were our lamentations; it was a serious problem. There was no one to take Leslie's place; all were fully committed. But in the simplest and most natural way, we expected God to reveal His will and His solution to us. As we prayed and talked together, the thought dawned upon one and another that possibly the Lord wanted to use *my* knowledge and experience to take up this work."

It was a battle for her. "It would mean that I must lay aside the work I loved, which had brought me into touch with people. Serving them had always given me much joy. It was obvious that the work was already far greater than the little team under Leslie could cope with. As he often said, 'it was like a snowball, with not enough hands to push it uphill.' "

The Lord confirmed His call and she obeyed, and God has greatly prospered her. "It is only possible," she adds, to give a glimpse into the magnitude of the work in the business side of things. There are administrative matters. There are the technical problems: censorship and selection of titles; forward quantity and general buying; repeat purchasing control. There is the need for knowing books, authors, publishers, etc. This involves long hours of reading and investigation. Then there is the receiving of goods, a very responsible job. The work also includes keeping up on records, correspondence, paper work, and besides all this, there are the weekly visits of publishers' representatives.

"In 1957 we were able to launch a training course in bookselling for our candidates. It is very comprehensive and is intended primarily for those who will be taking on the responsibility of a branch shop, an overseas center, or working in our London Mail Order Department.

"Things don't get easier as the years advance. But we are at liberty to say to Him: 'nevertheless I am continually with Thee'—we with Him and He with us—in all this back-room ministry. Some days seem humdrum and uneventful, when we feel that little has been done for our Master. It is then that we need to have a clear vision of the objective—the salvation and spiritual growth of men and women, and boys and girls, through the ministry of the printed page. The vision must be so clear that neither disappointment, difficulty, failure nor fatigue can dim it. We need to have the perseverance to continue, never letting the work of the Lord down. We know only too well what it is to suffer being tempted, to fail, to fall, or to falter in the fight. We need to be 'steadfast, unmovable, always abounding in the work of the Lord.' "

Dorothy Raxworthy occupies a little office on the fourth floor of 39 Ludgate Hill. When God puts you within four small walls, an office is a sanctuary and a humdrum job has the "spirit of glory and of God" resting on it. Dorothy, as could so many others, conveys the glow of it.

"I am otherwise known as Dorothy Grace," she says. "I was one of the seven prayed into the Mail Order Department. God spoke to me first of all about C.L.C. in 1951. By the autumn of 1952, He had made it so clear that I had to do something about it. I knew that I must obey. I was on vacation, staying at a Christian guest house. Each evening they had prayers, but I went into

town to attend Youth For Christ meetings. One evening
I felt convicted that I ought to stay for evening prayers
in the house. I didn't want to; I felt like a martyr by
staying. The room was full of old ladies. An elderly
retired missionary led the meeting. She read from 1
Chronicles 29 and when she got to verse 5, I knew God
was speaking to me: 'And who then is willing to con-
secrate his service this day unto the Lord?' At the close
we sang a hymn I've never liked very much, 'There's a
work for Jesus none but you can do.' Again I knew that
God was speaking to me about coming into C.L.C.
I went to bed that night with the words ringing in my
ears. In January 1953, I went forward in obedience to
God's call.

"Then doubts came. Big ones. And fear. Great blanket
walls of depression. I had seen something of the lives
lived by the folk at headquarters. I had seen, too, something of the amount of work being done at Ludgate Hill,
the late hours, the constant overtime, the lives of sacrifice
for the sake of Christ. Could I ever keep up such a pace?
In any case, just where would I fit into C.L.C.? I wasn't
trained in anything to do with books or bookselling.
I had been receptionist to my father, who was an optician.
One Saturday, while I was still a candidate at headquarters, I went home to visit my parents. Home pulled, as
it always has done with me. I said good-bye to Mother
at the door. She didn't see the tears which fell so fast as
I left her that I could hardly see to open the gate. As I
got on the bus I was still struggling to keep back the
tears. Had I made a huge mistake after all? What good
would I be in a mission like C.L.C.? Then I remembered
some letters I had in my bag, and fumbled for them. I
turned over the leaves of a magazine, which was among
the letters, but could not fix my mind on anything. I
closed the magazine. It lay upside down on my lap.
Suddenly, on the center of the back cover in large black
print, I read, 'Behold, I send an angel before thee, to

keep thee in the way, and bring thee into the place which
I have prepared.'

"The effect of these words was like an electric shock.
It seemed to me at that moment that the whole bus was
illuminated with God's presence. Everything seemed alight
with His glory. Surely the people in the bus must have
known God had spoken to me. Although I did not know
this until later, it was just then that the little group at
C.L.C. Headquarters were gathered together to wait
upon God for the seven new workers for the Mail Order
Department.

" 'The place which I have prepared'—I know that place
now and I believe with all my heart I am in it. It is
God's place for me. Have I had doubts since then? O yes!
Again and again. But in spite of all, I know that here
is my appointed job, doing secretarial and telephone
switchboard work. Here in a little office upstairs on the
fourth floor of 39 Ludgate Hill is God's place for me.
Here I realize His own wonderful peace in my heart.
Here I know the abiding presence of Jesus and here I see
something of His love and grace operating in the lives
of those around me. What a privilege! God has been
speaking to me again, revealing that His place for me
is the place of blessing and revelation. I have had experience of His love that I never would have had if I had
been disobedient when He first called me into C.L.C."

Dorothy Barnes had had library experience and was
accustomed to handling books and dealing with people,
so she was soon at home in the Ludgate Hill shop. Her
struggle was to accept a turn-down for overseas work,
and it took two years to find heart rest and a confirmation
of God's call to stay where she was. When Dorrie Brooking
moved into the Mail Order Department, Dorothy suddenly found herself in charge of the shop.

"One day Dorrie was there. Next morning she walked
in and straight upstairs, and I carried on," she recalls.
"I felt most inadequate. I thought to myself, 'I can never

be in this shop what Dorrie was.' But the Lord showed
me that it wasn't Dorrie, but Himself in her, and reminded me of His words to Joshua: 'As I was with Moses,
so I will be with thee.' Now I felt a real commission to
the job and a burden for the people of London. Each
year we look for an increase in sales. But how? Here I
realized again that being in a faith mission was not just
a question of doing a job and not being paid for it. Every
aspect of our lives is by faith. So we had to take sales
increases from the Lord by faith. And, praise Him, He
gave them."

Another of her special interests was the Christian
Unions in business firms. "All around us are thousands
of people working in offices. It isn't easy to contact them
in their homes or churches. They live within a fifty mile
radius of London. Most of the banks, insurance compa-
nies, etc., have a Christian Union group. I was thrilled
as the Lord opened up the way for us to set up booktables
at their meetings and weekend conferences. Introducing
books to them aroused their interest in Christian literature
and in C.L.C. As a result many have come into the shop
and asked advice about books, taking some to pass on to
non-Christians in their offices.

"The faith principle applies, too, in the matter of
staff. I was the only permanent worker in the shop and
I needed help. All I could do was look to the Lord. He
taught me many lessons in the exercise of faith in this.
Candidates passing through headquarters came for a few
weeks of training to prepare them for their future service
in a branch store or overseas. This meant a constant
change of personnel. Continually explaining the many
jobs to new personnel in the midst of a busy shop was
very wearing. It drove me to the Lord for strength and
patience. But I did enjoy the fellowship with each one
and the link it gave with the fields. Each had his own
contribution to make to the shop ministry, and would
have special contact with different types of people. Our

customers were so varied. We had many overseas visitors and foreign students, so were glad for the Continental candidates fluent in French and German. In conversation with a casual customer, a candidate might mention that he was going to a field, and the customer would learn, with surprise, that this wasn't just a bookstore, but a mission."

Even meals are prepared at Ludgate Hill. Being seven miles away from the living quarters in Norwood, the workers ate the midday meal at Ludgate Hill. One room was set apart on the fifth floor as a lunch room and another as a kitchen, with one of the staff, Ruby Dawney (nee Paddison), as cook. Not only was the cook a part of the faith staff, but the food came by faith as well. Then because of the pressure of work lasting often into the evening, they would get back to Norwood so late for the evening meal that it was finally decided to have that meal also at Ludgate Hill. And that meant the Lord sending in larger supplies.

"I had very little experience in the kitchen," says Ruby, "so it wasn't easy. It was just wonderful to see God undertake as I prayed over making things. Sometimes it turned out so good, I couldn't help laughing. I had a large family to feed, about twenty-six to thirty, or more at times. Some were visitors, some unexpected at the last minute, but it was wonderful to see how God made the meals go round.

"People often come in and bring gifts, and a nearby cooking school occasionally send in a lot of their products, cakes and so on, to the shop. So for sixteen years I have seen God's faithfulness in supplying for a hungry company, first one and then two meals a day!"

Actually, the latest advance in Britain has been in the Mail Order Department under the present British leader, Bob Hiley. The vision and output of Christian literature by mail, not merely inland but for the whole world, has greatly increased. This called for a new decision which was made after a year of prayer.

"Twenty-one years ago," says Bob Hiley, "when the C.L.C. opened the first small shop, the mail order service began with a list of seven names and addresses. The seven increased to seventy. It continued to grow year by year— to seven hundred, to seven thousand, to seventeen thousand. As orders poured into our London headquarters, tons of Christ-centered literature have poured into homes and hands in many lands. Today over one hundred lands and islands are being supplied from the London warehouse. The increased outreach naturally brings an increase in the amount of work to be done. Letters to be answered, invoices to be typed, accounts to be handled and telephone calls to be made and answered have all multiplied at the same tremendous pace.

"A year ago we in headquarters realized that to meet the need and to extend the work we would need larger mail order premises. Essential requirements were listed. We needed premises of approximately 10,000 square feet. To eliminate the time taken and the expense of traveling into the City it should be in the locality of our residential headquarters.

"Week by week, individually and in small groups, we brought this matter to the Lord in prayer. Days, weeks, months passed . . . then the answer came—9,000 square feet, and it was only a matter of yards from the headquarters of the mission. We had passed the gate daily and had never seen the building behind the wall. But late one afternoon a Crusade mother, busily engaged in office work, remembered the need of the family. Hurrying to the shop to buy a loaf of bread, she saw a man nailing a TO BE LET sign on the wall by the entrance to these premises. Instinctively she recognized God's moment. Even before the meal I was surveying the building and seeking to contact the agent.

"As negotiations were begun, the whole fellowship considered all that was involved. Obstacles loomed large and frightening. Manpower was at its lowest ebb and financial commitments were already heavy. To take on this new responsibility would involve us annually in thousands of pounds. If our overhead expenditure increased, would we not have less money to give to the overseas fields? Yet the Lord had told us to go forward and trust Him. Several times the staff met together for prayer and discussion. Some members of the fellowship were sure, others had doubts. Could He reveal His mind to so many people? Praise God He did! Each one had a different outlook, but all had the same uplook. The testimonies were thrilling to hear as one after another shared how God had spoken through His Word.

"On March 1, 1962, the key to these large new premises on Church Road, Norwood, in S. E. London, was ours. We believe that the ministry from this new mail order warehouse will reach out further than ever before."

Quotation on page 73 taken from *The Highway of Print* by Ruth Ure, page 239, Friendship Press, New York.

11

THE ARTIST IS EQUALLY NECESSARY

All types of work have their obvious importance in a literature ministry. The person. with art ability is no exception and his tasks are likely to be varied. The dressing of a window, the design of a book jacket, the cover and pictorial layout of a magazine, the type for article headings, the format of contents, all are tremendously important and can make the difference between a sale and a slump. God has had his man for this, the first of several for C.L.C.

Charlton Smith was one of a family of two brothers and three sisters, four of whom are in the W.E.C., and the fifth as good as in the Crusade through the way she and her husband use their home for the Lord and the work. Charlton, whose dramatic conversion was the beginning of his family's conquest by Christ, was an artist and wallpaper designer. His wife, Amy (now with the Lord), was also an artist and wallpaper designer. They attended a remarkable little mission hall in Acton Green, London, from which some twenty have gone into the Lord's service—most of them into W.E.C. and C.L.C. In the 1930's the call came to give up his assured position in England's leading wallpaper firm, together with his comfortable home, and to join the W.E.C. This was part of God's preparation for the birth of the C.L.C., because later Charlton was one of the two W.E.C. staff members who were constantly "getting at us" to expand our literature ministry. Soon after the start of the C.L.C., Charlton and Amy realized the use their gifts and training could have in a full-time literature ministry, and they became the first W.E.C. staff members to join the C.L.C. ranks.

It was Charlton who gave what was then the Evangelical Publishing House its new and present name. When C.L.C. was starting in North America, the name Evangelical Publishing House did not meet with approval. "The reason was," explains Ken Adams, "that there was a firm in Toronto known as Evangelical Publishers and our C.L.C. colleagues felt that our name looked too competitive. That sent us into a tail-spin, because we had hoped that this expanding organization would have the same name in all parts of the world. We tried to think of suitable substitute names. It was amazing the variety of titles that came to our attention! Those in North America were very ready to throw out our existing title, but they were not so ready to throw in a satisfactory title as an alternative! So we struggled for quite a long time, praying and watching to see what God would do.

"At our next annual conference the subject of a new title was on the agenda. Before we had begun discussion Charlton Smith had a sudden flash of inspiration.

" 'Ken, you keep talking about the need for Christian literature in the world. In your general comments you are constantly using those two words. Now, we are part of the Worldwide Evangelization *Crusade,* so we are a crusade handling Christian literature, isn't that right?'

" 'Yes,' I said, no pennies dropping yet!

" 'Well,' he continued, 'why don't we call ourselves the Christian Literature Crusade?'

"Once again there was recognition that God had spoken. We looked at each other and said, 'How stupid can we be? Why didn't we think of that? Here we are struggling with titles like Worldwide Bookroom and Conquest Publishing House—nothing ringing any bells—and now suddenly Charlton in his dreamy way says, "Why can't we call ourselves Christian Literature Crusade?" '

"The cautious British folks were not ready to use this title immediately, and concluded: this certainly sounds ideal but we ought to test it out a bit. For a year we'll just introduce this new name. We will still call ourselves Evangelical Publishing House, but we'll keep referring to the Christian Literature Crusade and see what sort of reaction we get from the Christian public.

"Not so our friends in North America! Immediately the suggestion reached them, it witnessed to their hearts that this was the right title and without further ado, they printed letterheads and put the name Christian Literature Crusade in the telephone book! The very next letter I received from North America was written on this C.L.C. letterhead. We shook our heads and said, 'These North American people! How they jump ahead!' There was a bit of correspondence back and forth, and we tried to rap their knuckles and tell them they were going too fast, but they rapped our knuckles and said, 'You're just going too slow!' Eventually Britain was fully persuaded that this new title was truly God-given so in 1946, the Christian Literature Crusade was adopted as the official name of the organization and we haven't had any more conferences since looking for another title."

"It was during my early days in W.E.C.," Charlton says, "that C.L.C. was born. I was interested from the very word 'go.' We sensed it was an answer to our prayer for the speeding up of worldwide evangelization. Ken would now and again approach me for a cover design or some guidance in printing. These requests increased until eventually my energy was getting spent in preparing drawings, and corresponding about such matters in my spare time. I was very reluctant to take up art work again, because the price of stepping out of a studio and the art life had been considerable. To be involved again was not easy because there was a temptation in it, but this new C.L.C. development was obviously an indication from the Lord that my art talent was to be used again—but this time in a different and more significant way. So as the demand increased, we heard the call of Christ to become involved with the C.L.C. team in the task of evangelizing through literature. A studio was established and all the equipment I had was put into it. More was added and soon we were preparing art work which was to reach the uttermost parts of the world. Not only was the home front catered for, but very soon requests for designs for books in other languages were coming our way. The work has so expanded that now the department flourishes with a staff of three.

"Another interesting fact is that in my former professional line I had been catering for a world market, preparing designs to meet the subtle different needs of different peoples. This also had been God's preparation, conditioning my mind as well as my heart to appreciate other people—their art, culture and approach. One is now sensitive to this need in preparing literature for different countries, a piece of work for France, for instance, being very different from a piece of work for Italy. When Amy and I were in the West Indies helping with the *Caribbean Challenge* magazine we again saw the importance of this. As we got closer to the people and better understood their thinking, we were able to design our work so that they felt the magazine was theirs and not something imported.

"The early window displays at Ludgate Hill were an adventure! These proved very effective in preaching the gospel and arresting the passers-by; in fact they developed so much interest that more than once we heard that these had been the subject of coffee-table-talk between strangers who had been attracted by the unusual approach to book display. Indeed, we don't say it boastingly, but it had an effect on the book trade. There was very little done in Britain in book display until we did something at Ludgate Hill. After that, some of the big firms began to do the same kind of thing—but I don't think they surpassed us, anyway. The Lord gave the inspiration to do this, and many have said that they became customers because of the book displays they couldn't resist. One window cleaner was so convicted by the display in the windows as he was cleaning them, that he went to the counter to ask how to be saved."

Ken Adams adds, "Charlton and others in the Art Department spend a lot of time creatively thinking through some of the ways in which to present new books attractively. For example, when a new title is published, such as *The Normal Christian Life,* by the Chinese author Watchman Nee, they would put a hundred or so copies in the window. Along with them there would be a model of a Chinese village, a plate of Chinese food or something similar to give a real Oriental atmosphere. Consequently there would be a steady stream of people looking in the windows hour after hour. Several publishers have asked us to make a display of a new title, offering to supply all the stock needed for the purpose. Often they would also supply the actual art work or at least the materials we would need for the display.

"This window-display ministry has been used over and over again to bless lives and challenge people; it speaks hour after hour, on the days we are closed as well as when we are open.

"The special display during the Billy Graham Harringay Crusade (his first in England) was referred to in *The Bookseller* (the journal of the British book trade), as the boldest and most effective display ever seen. We kept it in for twelve weeks because every time we were going to change it there were so many people looking at it we felt we had to leave it a little longer."

Hilda Miller, the first of Charlton's art assistants, assesses her job like this: "Helping to evangelize the world in the shortest possible time is the amazing work of some Crusaders behind the scenes. Tucked away in the top room up in 'The Hill,' I sat tearing up old newspapers into little pieces. Was I a Crusader at work, or was I what some may have thought, a bad case in need of psychiatric treatment? Some fellow-workers did venture to ask what I was doing, to which I could not resist the reply, 'Helping to evangelize the world in the shortest possible time.' Actually I was preparing papier machée to make a model head of the 'chocolate soldier' for a missionary exhibition. There were times when, playing around with such things, I seriously asked myself the question, 'Just what am I doing? Did I turn from home and loved ones to do jobs like this? Does God call people to such occupations?' Yet, the strange thing is, I can't get out of it. I've tried. Not so long ago, I really was right on the brink of leaving, to let go of art, to let it die, and to leave. My ability was seemingly gone, and the consciousness of a call gone also. But, just as I would have stepped out into some other work, God said, 'No!' He spoke in a way over which I had no conscious control, in the realm of the unconscious, by a dream. But I had no doubt in my conscious mind the next day what the dream meant. So maybe He does need some 'bods' who are good for nothing but to fill a space in the studio.

"Looking back I am amazed at the way God leads and keeps, and still leads on. Only since the beginning of this year (1962), God has been giving to me a vision to start silk-screen printing, confirming it by a seal and by His Word. Just what are the possibilities or the future for such work, I don't know. I just feel assured He is leading and will bring it all into being in His time."

12

THE EDITOR TELLS HER STORY

Miriam (Mim) Booth, Phil's wife, had the added problem of bringing two young children into the pioneer conditions of the early Colchester days. The rearing of missionaries' children is always a burning question, and I suppose opinions will always differ. What is the balance between the love, careful upbringing and the supply of material advantages of life which the parents naturally want to pour out on them and of which it hurts deeply to deprive them, and the total dedication to the call of a way of life which entails material sacrifice and often separations? Probably most missionary parents are in agreement, and certainly it has been the principle in the C.L.C., that the children should share their parents' life on a material level, even though in their early years the children may not understand why they do not have as much as other children. At the same time there is a desire to assure the children of the best possible educational preparation for their future lives, looking to God to make that somehow available to them. Not every missionary's child is a success story, no indeed—there are heartbreaks and disappointments—but I believe that by far the largest proportion of the children do come to know their parents' Lord and Saviour as their own, many following their parents into missionary service. That has been true of Phil and Mim's boy and girl, though the start looked unpropitious enough—David now continuing his studies on the human brain, after winning scholarships that took him through Oxford University, where he was a college representative of the Christian Union and leader of a missionary prayer group; Lois now completing her teacher training as a specially selected student for a year of advanced training.

In those early days Mim went through it as a young mother. But that was not all. C.L.C. wives and mothers are also Crusaders and combine with their home responsibilities some share in the literature work. "When we came to Colchester," says Mim, "we had been married for seven years and had a little boy and girl. The Lord said to me, 'I have chosen thee in the furnace of affliction . . .' and it was certainly not a 'flowery bed of ease.' For some months everything dried up on us. Financially, there were many tests. Physically, the children had one sickness after another. Our small boy was knocked down by a bicycle and badly cut about the lip. Dr. Stuart Harverson (now with W.E.C. in Viet Nam) who was staying with us at the time, stitched it up under the inadequate gas light in our attic bedroom. Because of the tremendous upheaval of the new life—no home of our own, a new school and the war-time bombing—our little lad had the worst attack of asthma he had known. Yet, even in that time of great anxiety, the Lord was so gracious. One morning, just before dawn, David called me, and putting his arms around my neck, told me he wanted to ask Jesus to live in his heart. How precious it was to guide him in this great transaction.

"As for the work we had come to do in the Crusade, where was it? My husband packed parcels of books in the basement for the home centers in Britain; and I did housework, often adding my tears to the water in the bucket. God certainly had much to teach us before He could entrust us with new service to Him for the lost souls of our land.

"During those early days, when we heard the ominous sound of the flying bombs coming nearer and watched

the lurid red light approaching across the night sky, I
used to rush upstairs to the room under the roof which
we shared with the children. I would kneel beside one
of their beds and just pour out my heart to God. What
peace, so close to that devilish noise, and how clearly
God's voice came through. During those times of prayer
He began to speak to me about my particular contribution
to the work of C.L.C. A cry had come from the mission
field: Oh, that someone would give us a magazine with
information about literature needs, current happenings,
books and so on. At the same time Ken Adams was bringing before our little fellowship the need for us to produce
such a paper. There was just nothing of this type available. Something in me rose to this challenge, and yet I
feared to grasp it. What did I know about such work?
And I had the children. Could a woman do such a job?
'Give me the title for such a magazine Lord,' I prayed,
'and then I'll know You mean me to do it.' He gave me
Floodtide. Summoning all my courage, I brought this title
to the fellowship and later to the Conference in London.
But it was turned down, 'quite unsuitable,' and I felt
they must know best. I went back to the Lord and asked
for another name. But no. 'I have given you *Floodtide*,'
He said. So I tried again, firmly declaring that I felt
such a title should be the one for our new magazine, link-
ing it up with the verse He had given: 'The earth shall be
full of the knowledge of the Lord as the waters cover the
sea.' To my amazement it clicked! 'Yes,' the folks said,
'that's the name. Now you have the vision, get on with
it'—the time-honored challenge of the Crusade was thrown
at me!

   "So I threw myself on the Lord. He brought to my
remembrance things I had unconsciously absorbed in
my previous business experience in a publishing firm;
a certain aptitude for art He translated into some idea
of how a magazine layout should look; and I set to work.
The magazine had to be done at night in our 'upper

room,' with the light shaded so that our children were not awakened. I worked on an old-fashioned marble-topped washstand. My files of material were in an old chest of drawers. The typing had to be saved up until the kitchen was available. All very well, but what was to go into the magazine? We began to realize how little was being done by evangelicals in the way of literature work in those days. Therefore most of the material for the first issues had to be gleaned from what we were doing ourselves through the bookstores in this country, together with items of challenge about the vast untouched fields before us.

"Yet, from the beginning, God blessed. The first number, which went out in the form of a printed newsletter, was acclaimed by many Christian friends as something that really met the need. Later, when we moved to London and the first issue of *Floodtide* appeared in January 1946, with two-color cover and glossy paper, folks were just thrilled. They certainly could not believe it was 'all my own work!' I knew only too well it was God working, as ever, through the frail 'earthen vessel.' Charlton Smith, whose art contribution to the magazine has continued through the years, designed the very attractive cover.

"One of the largest newsagents and booksellers in the country, for whom I worked when I was single, took copies to sell on their bookstalls. In their newssheet they printed a small paragraph introducing the new magazine. They were warm in their praise: 'This is something new in the way of Christian magazines, with its up-to-date format and attractive layout . . . ' Imitation is the best flattery—and in the following years we were to see a number of missionary magazines change their format to something similar in appearance.

"At the beginning, every address to which the magazine was sent had to be typed out separately, and I wore out one typewriter and made my fingers sore on this job.

Then we were able to buy a hand-operated addressograph which considerably lightened this task, although, as the circulation grew, it was still no easy thing wrapping and dispatching the thousands of copies, sometimes single-handed.

"When one launches into a ministry for God there is a battle. This magazine work was no exception. Every issue was sharply contested. In the early years when it was so difficult to get suitable material, the articles and items just had to be prayed in from nowhere it seemed! There were other battles too. Often the children would be ill, or I myself had to struggle on through some spiritual or physical attack. It was far from easy to prepare an issue for the printer when in the throes of a bout of enteritis or painful boils. Even during the birth of our third child the Lord wonderfully undertook, and with final instructions given from the hospital, I was able to see the magazine through in time.

"One afternoon, when I was busy preparing the next issue, pressing through to a dead-line date with the printer, my son came in from school in quite a dazed condition and collapsed in a chair. He had had a collision with another boy on the way home and had suffered a concussion. A nurse friend at headquarters came in to see him and told me he must be kept very quiet—for two weeks—and for the first day at any rate, in a darkened room. He lay there, practically unconscious. I sat at the table with my magazine material spread out, curtains drawn, light shaded, the boy laid out at my side—and prayed. Just then there was a gentle knock at the door and a head popped around the corner. It was Bessie Adams. She took in the situation at a glance and, 'Oh, my love,' she said, 'it's the devil.' Of course that was the crux of the matter. It was the devil. My prayer changed from beseeching to attack. I felt constrained to claim the victory in His Name and raised my arm, holding it aloft as though bearing an imaginary cross. Assurance flowed in and, sure enough, within an hour my boy was on his legs again—and the issue went on and reached the printers by the deadline."

Thelma Cooper, now editor of the *Caribbean Challenge* in the West Indies, helped in the editing for a time, and contributed a popular humorous feature, "Pepys Behind the Scenes"—a glimpse into some of the backstage activities of C.L.C. Since Phil and Mim Booth have now moved into the ministry of W.E.C. Radio Worldwide, Dorothy Barnes has become the British editor.

Both Australia and New Zealand now have their own supplements to the British magazine. North America has had its own edition for many years. Again the Lord has taken up women as editors, first Ruth Davis and now Bonnie Hanson. Bonnie, like Mim, accepted the commission, both as editor and artist, with no previous experience (except in art work). This magazine is printed on the C.L.C.'s own press in Fort Washington by yet another young woman, Virginia Walton, who taught herself printing and for a long time managed the press single-handed.

The blessing on *Floodtide* has continued through fifteen years and more. The book-review section, a voluntary contribution each issue by Gordon Chilvers, (which involves him in a heavy load of reading) has helped many. A number of literature workers are on the fields today through its pages. The pioneer of the "Challenge-type" magazine in Africa was stirred to make his start through *Floodtide*. Many have become literature agents in their own localities through it.

Requests to reprint articles come from magazine editors, and these are always gladly granted. Missionaries on the job also seem to appreciate the magazine. Typical is this word from Liberia, "I cannot tell you how much *Floodtide* means to me as it comes from time to time. I have received so much information and inspiration from the articles and news. Also it has put conviction and burden on my heart to do more in this line than we are doing now."

Not only are the contents appreciated but the format and style seem to meet with approval. "After receiving your recent issue I came to the conclusion that *Floodtide* is an outstanding publication. Each issue is visually exciting . . . excellent variety . . . a wonderful publication," writes one editor of a leading U. S. Christian publication. And from a literature group in South America, *"Floodtide* is certainly appreciated by all of us here and I just wanted you to know that its contents and layout are A-1 quality."

Requests for extra copies always encourage, for they usually indicate that a particular article has been helpful. One such inquiry came from a sizeable literature group in the States—"Because the Spring 1962 copy contained an article which proved to be so interesting . . . could we have an extra copy . . . the first installment of the article which impressed us so greatly is 'The World Struggle—And You.' We look forward to receiving the second installment." And another group was so blessed and impressed that they sent subscriptions for five members of the staff.

Perhaps the good wishes of another group best summarize the heart desire of all who work on the magazine . . . "we trust that its ministry will be increasingly effective in the days to come."

13

GETTING THE WORD OUT BY ALL MEANS

God often uses gifts and talents with which He has equipped us. But not always; in some cases it is the opposite. It is not a person's talents, but the person He uses. You never know what God will do. Of course the secret is we are all His, so He does exactly what He wants with us. Kathleen Redhead is one of the "opposite" examples, representative of so many others, as she, together with Muriel Worsfold, opened a British branch shop.

"I suppose I haven't offered to resign more than four times in the fifteen years I have been with the Crusade," Kathleen recalls. "But that is only normal for most of us! The Lord is able to knock us into shape and make us what He wants us to be and I think He must still be busy with me. I do praise the Lord for the fifteen years I have had. I came into the work for France. It was the need in Europe which attracted me. As I look back now, I wonder very much if it wasn't just because I liked French. It was one of my two good subjects at school. But the Lord has His own way of getting us into the place of His choosing and He used that to bring me into this Christian literature work. The other subject I was good in was music. The only time I've ever had need of it has been at an occasional prayer battery. I have never had any special need for French. I've come to the conclusion that God isn't tremendously interested in talents and gifts, but in a life given over to Him. So I have found myself in branch-shop work in Britain for fourteen years.

"I had the privilege—and I really mean privilege—of opening the Aberdeen center in northeast Scotland. Aberdeen is known throughout the world as the Granite City. It's also noted for its meanness. Of course the stories about Aberdonian meanness are quite untrue as nothing could be more wonderful than the generosities they have shown me these fourteen years. Anyway most of these stories are concocted by the Aberdonians themselves!

"Scotland is quite a different place from England. I'm afraid many of the Scottish people don't take a good view of the English. Possibly they have reason for that! A lady who was living in the same tenement was explaining to me how dirty and untidy one of the other tenants was and she finished up by saying, 'But, of course, she's English.' She forgot that I was too! But I must say I have enjoyed my years in Scotland.

"When our center was first opened the people were cautious and reserved. That is typical of the way they approach anything new. After about eighteen months they decided that C.L.C. wasn't some new heresy, and were really warm to us, opening their homes and hearts. Muriel Worsfold joined me after three months and the two of us have worked happily together since.

"It was a very small shop. Aberdeen is the center of the Scottish fishing industry on the east side. The harbor was always packed with little fishing boats on the weekends as the fishermen prepared to go to their homes, scattered all around the coast, some of them as far away as the Shetland Islands. Times have changed. They don't go home in their little boats now. They leave them in the harbor and get the plane for the weekend! These fishermen would come into the shop in their highnecked jerseys with their little black kitbags over their shoulders. When the fishing was good they would buy expensive Bibles and beautiful books for their children.

"We also had our language to learn. Aberdeen has a very strong dialect, not only accent but dialect. There are lots of strange words. Until we began to learn the language, we just didn't know what they meant. But we got into the way of it and over the years, have grown to love and respect the people of the northeast. We have found wonderful friendship and fellowship among them.

"Scotland doesn't have a lot of big cities. There are many scattered villages and small towns inland as well as all the little fishing villages along the coast. Therefore we soon came to the conclusion that the great need was to be mobile. When the Lord showed this to Muriel and me, we began to pray. Then we wrote to London saying that we needed a vehicle of some kind. London replied, 'O.K. fine, you go to it. It's your vision.' So that was that. It was our vision! Well, we went on praying, now adding a definite request for £460. It really did seem fantastic. Why should God give £460? Yet God had given us an urge to believe Him. For eighteen months we prayed and believed, and then the Lord sent us a gift of £300. When it came—we wept. We were so overwhelmed that the Lord should send this to us. When we got over the wonder of it we took it back to Him and said, 'Lord, we thank You for the £300; but it isn't enough. It's £460 we need.' Not many weeks later we received another gift for £160. Then we did have a day of rejoicing! We managed to get a very nice Ford van which had only done 3,000 miles. A Christian friend made some beautiful shelves and another friend who was a sign painter helped us. Soon the happy day came when our van drew up to the door, fitted out with shelves, beautifully painted, and the sign CHRISTIAN LITERATURE CRUSADE, BOOKS THAT RADIATE LIGHT attractively painted on both sides.

Now we were ready to begin our mobile ministry in earnest. We spent most of one afternoon and night packing the van with beautiful books of all kinds. As we set out the next day, it was pouring with rain but we weren't to be turned back. First, we went to the little town of Gardenstown on the coast of Bannffshire. I feel it was just the Lord encouraging us at the beginning of our ministry for that day we sold £42 worth of Bibles and books in that little place of less than 1,000 population. The people were greatly interested in the van. One brought another. They in turn would tell us of others who they felt would be interested in buying something.

"But it hasn't all been like that. It's lovely to have highlights and success, but there are times when the going has been tough. Perhaps we wouldn't sell £2 worth in a day. Every job has to start from the foundation, and we saw that if this mobile work was really going to make its mark, we would have to be willing to put in the spade and do the pioneering. This we did and it has gone on from strength to strength. Very soon we had a great book full of addresses of people who expected us to call on them, though we couldn't be there more than once a year with such a large area to cover. It was wonderful the way the Lord opened hearts and homes and promoted interest, sometimes in unlikely people.

"We began to be expected each Christmas season, and if one year we missed somebody who should have been called on, we got into trouble later! We worked six days a week from 9 in the morning until 10 at night to get the Christmas rounds done. It was wonderful to see all the books, cards and calendars bearing the Word of God going out. We wouldn't have done it for anybody but the Lord.

"In the spring people were not as interested in books, so we decided to make a systematic call on the ministers. This was quite a tough job. We never knew what sort of a reception we would get. He might be amiable. He might be argumentative. He might be just plain uninterested. But what an interesting time we had. Some bought quite freely.

"One day we called at a large manse which had a long path lined with beautiful flowers leading up to it. Somewhat overawed we wondered what sort of a reception we would get. The minister came to the door and was quite amiable at first. but when he discovered we were trying to sell books, he froze immediately. He turned his back, saying, 'If there is ever anything I want, I'll get in touch with you.' So we went back down this long drive, feeling a little bedraggled. However, we committed it all to the Lord. We had several addresses to call at in that town. One of them was a Sunday school superintendent. He turned out to be extremely interested and said, 'You are the sort of people I've been looking for for a long while. I want some supplies for my Sunday school teachers.' The outcome was that he spent £25. Then he said, 'My, I'll have to handle this carefully with my minister. He doesn't know I've spent all this money.' We happened to say quite casually, 'And who is your minister?' It was the very one we had visited earlier! So the Lord has His own way of guiding. If we don't get in the front door, it is sometimes quite possible to get in the back.

"We had also the opportunity of encouraging some of the country ministers. Many of them were soundly converted men, but over the years, perhaps through lack of response, they may have been discouraged. We found some were really glad to talk with us of their difficulties. We tried to minister, not only with the books but with the Word of Life. Very humbly we praised God for these opportunities.

"Of course, we were out in all kinds of weather, and in the northeast corner of Scotland there can be some pretty rough winters. I don't know whether or not a woman is the one to go round in a van on dark winter nights on roads she doesn't know. Yet God kept us safe and His hand was upon us for good always.

"One day when I got into the open country I found the van was swaying all over the road. I suddenly realized I was driving through a full-scale gale. Great branches of trees were being hurled across the road and I began to get a little nervous. Then down came the rain in torrents.

Finally the wind rose to such a shriek that it almost blew me into the ditch as it ripped off the wipers from the windshield. I had to drive five miles to the nearest little town. It was evident that God had His hand upon me that time. The evening newspaper told of cars being blown off the road. We praise Him for all the thousands of pounds worth of books that have gone out into our area in season and out of season, through the mobile work."

"Sandy" and Ella Sanderson are the two in C.L.C. who can genuinely be called "C.L.C. gypsies." Unlike the mobile work in Scotland which was carried on as part of the Aberdeen store ministry, the Sandersons' vision was that of a total mobile ministry six days a week and the whole year around. But their call was to be severely tested. Many get a call, but few stick to it, especially when their chief opponents are their own co-workers! No suitable vehicle was available for such a ministry and until one was forthcoming nothing further could be done. This was an obvious challenge to faith and was accepted accordingly. Meantime some practical experience in other aspects of the literature work was to be gained through service in one of the bookstores so the Sandersons were appointed to the great industrial city of Birmingham. This was completely against their natural desires. It was a test indeed. At first they worked with rebellion in their hearts, but the Lord met them. As they got more deeply involved and saw the vast needs of Christless men and women, and shared in meeting that need, they were sincerely thankful for the six years of bookstore ministry. But the vision burned brightly and each year at the Annual Conference they presented their case and tried to get their release!

In due course the vehicle came. The very first gift towards it was five shillings and came from an old-age pensioner. Other gifts, small and large, kept coming until a total of £500 made the purchase of the mobile unit possible. No one in C.L.C. had experience in this type of mobile work and the Sandersons were just advised to "get the pattern from the Lord" and go to it. The break came with an invitation to Mid-Wales, with the suggestion of a bookstall in the local market. "We had never considered this method," says Sandy, "and had no experience of market work, but trusting in the Lord, off we set.

"On arrival at Welshpool, the market was already busy and all the stalls occupied, except one, and the reason was obvious—it had no canopy and one leg was broken. It seemed hopeless, but we sought out the Market Superintendent who said there was only one stall left—and yes, it was the broken-down one. If we could use it we could have it for the day! Jostled by staring crowds, we pulled the stall around to face the main street, put a box under the corner in place of the broken leg, and although we had no cover and snow was threatening, we began to set up our books. The effect was terrific! Before we could make anything that looked like a display, the crowd was around the stall exclaiming with delight at the Bibles and variety of evangelical books. They'd seen nothing like it before. It was a thrill to us on our first day to find such enthusiasm, and each day that week it was the same. One lady told us that in thirty years she could not recall such a stall in their market.

"From markets we were led to visit agricultural shows which attracted large crowds of people who, having paid for admission, wander around looking at every stall, accepting free literature at each. This makes it easy to approach people and engage them in conversation, and then pass on gospel tracts. It is thrilling to see the Lord answer prayer in sending needy souls to us. Amid all the display of material things our little stall, often the only evangelical witness among 400 trade stands, becomes a true 'Bethel.' We have to be ready for anything since our contacts range from the honest seeker to the rank unbeliever; from anxious souls to absolute atheists or agnostics. The Lord proves Himself sufficient in all situations. At one show an old man, after looking at the books, said he was interested in missionary work. We told him about our Crusade, and at the mention of C.T. Studd his eyes lit up and he said, 'I heard Mrs. Studd once in Swansea. I'll never forget that meeting.' When we showed him the book with Mother Studd's photo, he was thrilled and bought it at once. Two or three minutes later he was back and handed us £5 with instructions to put it in our funds. He told us that he was a pig farmer and that out of each litter of pigs he 'raised some for the Lord'!"

There have been times in some markets when the Sandersons toiled all day and saw very little for their efforts; days when the wind caught their most expensive calendars and blew them into the muddy roadway; occasions when it seemed that the local population did not even read the daily paper, let alone Christian books. How could the workers discover, and then, by spoken testimony and printed word, try to meet the spiritual need of such people if they were not willing to go to these places as pioneer literature missionaries? And pioneer is the right word.

"We have also been invited to have bookstalls at gospel campaigns," continues Sandy, "and as we team in with the evangelist, as well as handling the books, we find wonderful opportunities of presenting the challenge of literature evangelism. One result is that local representatives, who caught the vision through seeing the C.L.C. mobile unit in action, are now doing a grand job in their own areas. This is also the case at such conventions as Keswick, where the public sees us on the street with a vehicle which is in use twelve months of the year, and not something specially 'got up' for the occasion. At our Youth Crusade camps we set up our stall and enter fully into the life and ministry of the camp, and are thus able to present the claims of literature and the missionary challenge to the young people.

"This does not mean that all goes smoothly with the Mobile Section; in fact it has been a real battle to keep it going. Road hazards, weather, stock control, long journeys, late nights, irregular meals, a strange variety of beds and welcomes, have all combined to cast us upon the Lord. Often after a cold wet day in a quiet market, we've wondered just what was being accomplished. On one occasion we were physically assaulted; but I think our biggest test came through the C.L.C. fellowship itself.

"We had been making Leeds, Yorkshire, our base but in 1960 felt that we should be available to the whole country and not confined to Yorkshire, so we asked the Lord for a house trailer to make us fully independent in areas where we have no contacts. The Lord is good, and by October we had become possessors of two trailers! We kept the four-berth one and in the Spring of 1961 we gave up the accommodation in Leeds and became fully mobile."

The most severe tests on our obedience of faith are usually those nearest to us: Jesus' parents and disciples, Paul's companions who would stop him from going to Jerusalem, C.T. Studd's closest friends. They think they know best what it will mean to us. God does not even mean them to see as we do. Their opposition and questionings will shake what can be shaken, so that that which cannot be shaken may remain; for the inner call of a Divine commission is always to an individual, and must be proved and demonstrated in some lonely testing ground, such as Luther's "Here I stand. I can do no other"; and Esther's "If I perish, I perish." So in this wider mobile calling, "we did not feel," says Sandy, "that the fellowship of the Crusade was wholly behind us, and that brought discouragement and frustration. We were asked to take over another aspect of mobile work, and although assured that it would only be temporary, we felt that our 'baby' was to be systematically starved out.

"Our feeling was that God had given us this ministry

and the pattern, and if C.L.C. did not accept it fully, they were refusing something God had given. So we very seriously began to ask the Lord where He would have us go when we pulled out of C.L.C. In previous times of difficulty we had often talked of 'getting out,' but then we knew that we'd be running out of God's will. This was different. We knew the will of God and felt that the Crusade was not willing to accept it. Finally we went to headquarters and, in an atmosphere of wonderful, loving fellowship, we were able to get the whole position clarified. Out of our deliberations came the full pattern of mobile work in the United Kingdom, with perfect harmony on all sides. How gracious is our Lord.

"Some concern was expressed about our not having a real 'home.' The trailer was not really equipped for winter use, not having a heating stove. We really felt we could not continue in such conditions and spent a time in prayer. Just as we finished there was a knock on the door. There stood the farmer in whose yard we were parked. He brought a convector-type heater which he said we were to use as long as we were there, and that there was an ample supply of kerosene in the garage, so we were to keep it on day and night. Did we praise the Lord! We have since been given a heater of a similar type and lived comfortably in the trailer with seven inches of snow around us, and the temperature a good bit below freezing."

14

IF THINE ENEMY HUNGER

In the beginning days it was the national vision which filled the horizon of the young C.L.C.—and that seemed big enough. But, as Ken said, "The Lord doesn't usually give us a blueprint and spell out in detail all that is going to happen during the next twenty years. Rather step by step as there is an enlarging of capacity, and as we can take more responsibility. He shows us something more and uses different ways to do it."

The news of the happenings in Britain spread to W.E.C. centers in other English-speaking lands. First Australia, and then North America, caught the vision and moved into action. The horizon now expanded to include evangelical literature, not for the British Isles only, but for the English-speaking world also. And that again was only a further build-up to the real breakthrough —the foreign program, literature to the whole world. A young mission can talk in terms of a world outreach, but to do it and be a world crusade with finances, stocks, dedicated personnel, many bookstores in other lands— that is another matter. God led this little literature mission on by such gradual stages, yet each one involving a further stride and leap of faith, that it was almost as if they woke up to find themselves worldwide—almost as if they were tricked by the Spirit into a world commission with a world ministry and the constant acceptance of a world burden. Yet it really was stage by stage and step by step.

"God now began to show us," says Ken, "the possibilities of a wider field of ministry. It came about in a very simple way. While in Colchester we had received a number of orders from North America for W.E.C. literature but, because of the war, it was extremely difficult to get shipping for non-essentials, and literature was considered a non-essential. Consequently these orders were put at the bottom of the pile, and there they stayed. By this time the Lord had brought Phil and Mim Booth to us.

"But first let me give the setting of those pioneer days. On one side of the room, and just behind the door, was Phil's 'desk' which was nothing more than a rather rickety table made secure by being attached to 'Pa Why's' table, which in turn, again for security reasons, was nailed to the wall. On the opposite side near the window was my desk which, if my memory serves me correctly, was the only genuine piece of office furniture C.L.C. had to its name. Opposite me was Leslie Fitton's corner. The four of us worked together in close fellowship in this one-windowed room measuring appoximately 12' x 15' and known by the dignified name of 'General Office'!

"On several occasions we had talked a little about the need to develop an information bureau regarding foreign literature. We felt it would be good if we had on display a selection of books and pamphlets in French, German, Italian and so on, and Phil, almost as a hobby, had been trying to get this information and stock together. Then one day I came upon these pending orders from North America at the bottom of the pile and I got a bright idea. I put them on Phil's desk and said, 'Phil, you're the Foreign Department, wouldn't you like to solve some of these problems?' A day or two later a letter came from overseas inquiring about literature for another country and I handed this over to Phil saying, 'You're the Foreign Department, Phil, you'd better handle this.' So once again, in a very unpremedidated way, we sort of stumbled along and came up with the right answer! The Foreign Department was now in being and Phil was the overseas secretary.

"So the overseas work began to take shape: First to link the English-speaking world together supplying books to and from North America, and later to Australia, New Zealand, etc.: Then to make a serious attempt to supply information about literature in other languages. But the vision was enlarged further. We began to recognize that there were people in areas other than English-speaking who needed Christian literature. In a personal way this conviction came to me through a visit from a missionary from North Africa. He came to bring greetings from my sister and brother-in-law who were missionaries there. Looking at the well-stocked shelves he commented, 'You have a wonderful selection of books here, especially for war-time; other shops seem quite empty in comparison.' And then with emphasis and conviction he continued, 'If only we had a bookshop like this in North Africa.' I expressed surprise and asked him if he really thought there was scope and need for a Christian bookshop in North Africa. He assured me there was. I was nonplussed. Nothing further was said on the subject. But this I know —his challenge never left me. God used that 'casual' comment to awaken in me a consciousness of there being a literature need in non-English-speaking countries. I was to meet this challenge again, but from a different angle and under different circumstances.

"By the time we moved to Ludgate Hill, Phil had gathered a sample stock of literature in the major European languages, mainly from Switzerland. By now the war was over. In the Allied Army of Occupation in Germany there were many keen Christian fellows. They appreciated the hospitality of the people but couldn't speak the language too well and felt that if they could find some books to give them, these would be a permanent expression of their appreciation and a token of Christian fellowship. So when on leave they came to C.L.C. at Ludgate Hill expecting us to have all the supplies they needed! We didn't, but it challenged us. Then we began to make contact with students from different countries and of different languages who were studying in London. These opportunities seemed to indicate that we should have a stock of books in other languages in a corner of the store, and so encourage some of the various nationalities to come in.

"One weekend I had meetings in Chatham where we had one of our bookstores. The chairman of the Saturday night meeting, I found out later, was the Chaplain for several prisoner-of-war camps in Southern England. During my address I told of the hopes of C.L.C. to publish and distribute Christian literature in foreign languages. I also mentioned the samples of books we were gathering for our library of references. After the meeting he said, 'I am particularly interested in your reference to your literature plans. What do you have in German?'

" 'Brother,' I said, 'we haven't anything in German. We do have a few sample copies of German literature, but what I've been sharing with you tonight is really only a vision. We're not doing anything!'

"The next day he came to the bookstore for a chat. Soon he was pouring out his heart. 'Mr. Adams,' he said, 'I've been greatly concerned since I heard you speak last night. That message has been just getting hold of me. I am responsible for several camps in which there are literally thousands of Germans, and some Italians. If only we could have Christian literature in these languages for these fellows. Many are well educated—doctors, lawyers, university students, men with brains and keen minds. Here they are just rotting away, as it were, with nothing to do. We need books, good books and plenty of them. We need them at once!'

"Two days later he came to Ludgate Hill and when he saw the Bibles and the fifteen or so titles in the

German language, he nearly jumped out of his skin with excitement. It was as though he had stumbled upon a gold mine! 'Let's have a word of prayer,' he said, and did that brother pray!

"It wasn't long before he added action to his prayer. He arranged for us to see three key people. One was a bishop who was the official representative of the British Government for the religious welfare of the prisons. A second was a German doctor representing the Germans. Phil Booth saw both of these men and they were enthusiastic about our plan to provide reading material for the camps. But our real problem was not yet solved. Finally we were given an appointment with a member of the House of Lords in the British Parliament. Phil Booth was ushered into his office and told his story. He produced his array of books and began to do a bit of salesmanship, reminding the good lord how Hitler had destroyed the youth of Germany through his book *Mein Kampf*. He suggested it was now our responsibility to rebuild these young people by giving them the tenets of the Christian faith. He showed real interest, and then Phil came to the point. 'We have a problem. We are unable to get an import license to bring the books into the country from Switzerland.'

" 'How much do you want?' came the inquiry.

" 'We would like a £500 license for this year,' calculated Phil.

" 'Well,' he said, 'I will see what I can do for you and will certainly refer it to the President of the Board of Trade.' Then he pulled out his wallet and gave Phil a five-pound note as a contribution to the work of the Crusade.

"Of course Phil brought the news back to us and said, 'Now we must pray this thing through, it's in this good lord's hands!' Within ten days prayer was answered and we had the import license in our hands, but a mistake had been made. Instead of giving us £500 for one year, they gave us £500 per *quarter,* so we now had an import license for £2,000 worth of literature from Switzerland for each year! There was much rejoicing and, as you can appreciate, our chaplain friend was just thrilled. It was not long before the books began to come in and plans were set up for distribution to the prisoners-of-war."

Now also there were ample stocks for the Occupation soldiers to take with them on their return to Germany after leave. Then came a more specific challenge direct from Germany. An R. A. F. Chaplain in Germany read a copy of *Floodtide,* where it spoke of the plan to open bookstores around the world. He offered to supply someone to look after a bookshop in Lubeck in northern Germany if we would supply the literature. Neither he nor the C.L.C. had any money available. However, within a few days, after he and Phil Booth had knelt together in Phil's office and prayed, a gift of £250 came, and the first big consignment was shipped out through government channels. It arrived just in time for a German pastors' retreat. Before the weekend was over, every piece of literature had been sold, and it had been meant for a bookstore! Immediately the word came back, 'Send us more, send us more!'

"What could we do?" continues Ken. "We were faced with a new challenge. Our resources were being severely tested. Another consignment of books was sent and the Lubeck store opened with a mere trickle of literature. I had been away on meetings. When I came back to headquarters, I asked Phil how things were going over in Europe.

" 'Tremendous,' he said, 'simply tremendous. The possibility of two other stores has come into the picture, in Oldenburg and Hamburg.'

" 'Praise the Lord,' I said, 'that's wonderful.' But Phil wasn't nearly so enthusiastic.

" 'Ken,' he questioned, 'what can we do? We've exhausted all of our stock and resources. What's the good of trying to open two new bookstores when we're not keeping the supplies moving efficiently to meet the need of the one? It seems silly.'

" 'Can't we get more stock?' I asked.

" 'Yes, we can,' acknowledged Phil. 'There is stock in Switzerland, but we'll need money.'

"From past experience we knew what to do in such circumstances—tell the Lord about it. So we agreed to share the facts in the regular Tuesday night prayer meeting, and Phil put the need at £1,000. This we recognized as a direct challenge to faith. The question was, could we rise to it? One by one spoke and said, 'Let us take the money from the Lord,' and there was a real rise of faith in our hearts. That was a step in the right direction, but what about the time factor? It seemed clear that we should act without delay. We agreed, therefore, to ask the Lord for an adequate provision before the end of the month. Unitedly we went to our knees. The course before us was clear. In simple language and in full assurance of faith we prayed, 'Lord, we are asking You for an outright gift of £1,000 to help us meet this need in Germany.' And then we added this word, 'Please Lord, may we have the money by the end of this month.' A flood of assurance led us immediately into a time of praise and rejoicing. No longer did we pray 'Please give.' Instead we said a simple 'Thank You, Lord, for the supply which is now on its way.'

"To faith the next step was obvious, if you have it, then use it. But the days slipped by and there wasn't any sign of the money. During that time Phil said to me, 'Ken, what do you think? Shall we take action now or just wait until the money comes?' We agreed that since 'Faith is the substance of things hoped for' we should spend what we have by faith, and that meant sending the orders to Switzerland. We would get the usual thirty-days credit and as the money would be in hand by the end of the month we would be able to pay our bills in

March. So we wrote out these orders and it wasn't long before most of the money had been spent, and we still hadn't a penny of it in hand.

"The action of faith was to be applied further. Miriam Booth, as editor of *Floodtide,* wrote an article for the March issue about this new launch into Germany. The proofs came from the printer about the twentieth of the month. Still there was no money. Mim brought the proofs to me and said, 'I really ought to be getting these back to the printers. What are we to do?'

" 'You're the editor,' I reminded her, 'what are *you* going to do?'

" 'I don't know,' she answered, 'we don't have the money and this article says, "Rejoice with us at the wonderful gift of £1,000 that God has sent us to forward the work in Germany." '

" 'Well,' I asked, 'have we got it or haven't we?'

"She hesitated and said with confidence, 'Yes, yes, we have.'

" 'Then if we have it, we might as well tell the people,' was my reply. 'As far as I'm concerned go ahead and put it in.' And in went the final proofs—now there was no turning back.

"I must admit that by this time we were getting a little bit shaky. It was now the 25th or 26th of the month. I had been opening the general mail and there was no sign of any financial deliverance. All that was left were bills, invoices and a letter from the bank. It was just a printed form so, as far as I was concerned, would not have any significance in relation to our need. I scanned it casually. 'We wish to inform you that we have today (there was credit and debit together and they had scored out the debit), credited your account with £1,000.' I was immediately alert—and confused! For a moment I couldn't think what credit was—my bookkeeping was pretty feeble in those days! I thought, 'credit,' does that mean in or out?! Then I looked again, more carefully, and still thinking out loud reasoned, 'Yes, credit, that's in, isn't it?!' This conclusion was fully confirmed when I noticed at the bottom a typed-in note which read, 'The donor wishes to remain anonymous but expresses a desire that this money be used for your work in Germany.' Now I was convinced! I went out of that office like a shot, hunted for Phil and shared the good news with him and the rest of the staff. I can assure you that the telephone began to ring.

"That's the way the Lord gave us an indication of the sort of thing He wanted us to do in building the C.L.C. We were to act in direct response to His revealed will and expect Him to meet the bills. Thousands more have gone into the work since then, not only in Germany but in other parts of Europe. Today the C.L.C. operates in six European countries. We have moved on from that first bookstore in Lubeck to more than a dozen shops and to mobile units and to publishing in several European languages.

But, as we have seen, the specific challenge to a widespread overseas ministry came first by meeting the need of foreigners right on our own doorstep, and then the immediate need just across the North Sea. We yet had to lift up our eyes to see the needs of the people of Africa, the Far East, South America and elsewhere. But that was to come fairly quickly."

15

CALL OF THE CONTINENT

From the early days of the work on the Continent, Charlton Smith was a visitor to the various countries. The fact that Amy, his wife, was partly Swiss, made them feel in a special way that they belonged to both sides of the Channel. "I found three little buildings huddled together in a vast expanse of ruin in a severely bombed section of Hamburg," writes Charlton of that first visit to Germany. "The C.L.C. missionary, Bob Shaffer, had acquired one of them. There was a shop and a back room for his stock, office, sleeping and eating. Before he could use it he had had to clean up three years accumulation of dirt!

"I arrived twenty-four hours before the shop was to be opened. Bob gave me a window-dressing job to do. There was no display material, no bookstands, only some old wire which we found on the premises. This I clipped into lengths and shaped into bookstands. Then I covered boxes with paper and began to build up a display behind the shattered window. At about 3 o'clock in the afternoon he suggested we'd better eat. As we hadn't stopped since breakfast I quickly agreed. We obtained water from a neighbor's tap and washed our hands in a bowl. Bob had loaned me an old jacket to work in. The elbows were worn through and the sleeves frayed. I was going to put on my decent one, but he said the old one would look more appropriate where we were going.

"Off we went, stumbling over the rubble. Soon we

popped through a hole in the wall which I imagined led to another lot of ruin, but was surprised to discover a roof over the walls, and a little window. This was the eating house. The plank table, where we ate our bowls of stewed vegetables and gravy, had been fixed by brackets all around the wall. We mingled with folks whose expressions suggested frustration and distress. Bob explained that he used to eat on the boulevard, but the cost was twice as high and he was twice as far from the people he wanted to reach for Christ. My heart thrilled to hear this.

"The next morning the shutters were raised and the window display opened to public gaze for the very first time. The people passing through the ruins would now see color, in contrast to the drabness of the broken city. That first day the sales were precisely one post card, that's all! Out of that tiny beginning grew the Hamburg center which now stands on one of the main streets of a rebuilt city.

"Some time later, Bob, Amy and I paid a visit to the German-speaking territory of Austria. We started from the city of St. Gallen in eastern Switzerland, the home of a prayer-partner of C.L.C., Freda Ferber. It was early November. The first winter snow had fallen, plenty of it, and deep. We spent Sunday in that Christmas-card country. The pine trees were laden with snow, and the hills a foot deep with the same whiteness. We were relaxing and waiting on God because after breakfast the next day we were going to commence a six-week journey that would be true adventure and it proved to be a greater adventure than we first imagined. Breakfast over we wrapped in our heavy coats and prayerfully stepped out into the winter morning. The Volkswagen was loaded down to the springs. The three passengers were tucked in between the packages, and the personal baggage was on the roof rack. We headed east in the direction of Austria and very soon we were near the border. Snow was falling fast, visibility was poor. Our prayer was that we would get through customs without difficulty. Books are highly taxed in Austria. On this occasion we couldn't afford to pay a tax, and not only that, we weren't doing a commercial piece of work, but were taking in 'living' literature to 'dying' men. The proceeds from the sale of these books were to be banked in Austria and left there as a foundation for the beginning of the C.L.C. in that country.

"Very soon the barrier across the road brought us to a halt. We waited while the customs officer came from his little hut. It took a bit of courage to leave his hut; a blizzard was upon us now. It would have taken a bit of courage to leave the car, because even to open the door meant we would fill up with snow. The customs officer was a shrewd man, very kind, but he didn't even ask us to get out. He examined our passports and asked questions about our load. We admitted we had some literature and handed him a tract. He was anxious to get back to his stove, and so he opened the barrier and let us through. God had sent a blizzard to cover us up! We praised the Lord.

"For eight hours we traveled over mountain roads, dangerous with deepening snow. The plows had been at work cutting trenches through which we traveled like an insect burrowing in the soil, for the snow was as high as the car. Eventually we found ourselves coasting downward to the valley below and the attractive Alpine town of Innsbruck where we stayed for the night. After the coffee-and-roll breakfast we wiped the snow off the car and moved on again into more dangerous and difficult country. But we couldn't go through by road so we put the car on a train and traveled through the railroad tunnels. When we emerged it could have been the North Pole as far as appearances were concerned.

"By evening we reached Salzburg where we were expected for a meeting. We were in the largest hall in town and a nice sized company had gathered. It was a thrill to prepare a large booktable and display all our wares. The people gathered around the table and were even impeding progress in arranging it. They weren't buying, they were just curious as if it were an exhibition. Meeting-time came, but nobody sat down. The leader called them and we took our places on the platform, but it was only after much persuasion that they came and were seated. As soon as the service was over nearly all the people dashed back to the booktable again. It was like a bargain basement for the counter had just the things they were looking for. They were beginning to buy now, and it was quite late before we even began to pack up because the people just hung on until they were fully satisfied. We were thrilled of course, and amazed that they were so enthusiastic.

"For a few days we used a small hotel as a base from which to visit other nearby towns. Night by night these meetings were very profitable, as we preached and sold the books. I had never seen enthusiasm like that before. The people weren't just glad we had books, they were excited. When those who had no money with them discovered that their opportunity for buying would pass because we were moving on next day, they were distressed and openly said so. The concern was noticed by the leaders in each place, so they quickly arranged for the people to pay them later. There were two groups of people, one with money at the booktable making purchases, and the other lining up to have the details of their requirements taken. These books would be left behind and the pastor would deliver them to the customers when they produced the cash. But that wasn't our concern. Our burden was that they should receive the books.

"One night, standing back watching this amazing scene of the two groups of people, without one disinterested soul in the company, I said to the pastor, 'It's amazing to see the people so excited about these books.'

" 'They are buying the first spiritual book of their lives,' he replied.

" 'The first spiritual book of their lives?' I queried, for the people were not young—thirty would probably be the youngest.

"As he saw my surprise he went on, 'Don't you realize this is the first time we've had evangelical books in Austria since Hitler came to power?'

"As this tempo of selling continued in town after town, we had to ration the books or our supply would have been exhausted too soon. The contacts we made were amazing—some were poor, some were from comfortable positions, some were displaced persons. To see such enthusiasm for the books and have such fellowship with the few believers was an inspiration.

"One Sunday morning we arrived outside what seemed to be a bit of a ruin, but later we learned it was a place of worship being built by refugees from Eastern Europe. They had formed a little colony and were erecting the building from war-damaged material. We walked over the building site and into a hall at the back. It was cozy and warm and packed tight with people. At the end of the day, a young lady of about twenty-five told us we were going to sleep at her place that night. She joined us in the little car and directed us as we drove through the streets in total darkness. We learned that the lights on the hill beyond were in Russian territory. The Russions occupied great portions of Austria at that time.

"Soon we arrived at quite a large building which we couldn't discern very well in the darkness. We entered through large doors, and walked up wide concrete stairs. There were some bicycles at the side of the stairs. We passed on up to another corridor a floor higher. There were doors in every direction. When our door was opened, we anticipated a living room, but not so, it was a bedroom. As we stood holding our bags because there was hardly room for our feet and our luggage, we were somewhat dazed to find ten beds in the room, seven already occupied with a mixed company. It was wholesome and clean enough, but the situation was a little delicate because of the folks already there, beside our hostess, Bob, Amy and myself. She seemed a little concerned because we didn't respond heartily to their genuine hospitality. We remarked about their graciousness and generosity, but that really didn't solve the problem.

" 'Won't it do?' she asked.

" 'Well, the problem, as I see it,' I broke in after some hesitation, 'is that there are only three beds and there are four of us.' I thought it better to plunge right into the situation than just be embarrassed by it.

" 'Oh,' she answered, 'that's all right. We've another sleeping room and I'm going there.' "

"Later on, we found out that this was a displaced persons' camp, and thus we were able to experience first-hand how many had to live in those difficult post-war years. We slept there that night without screen or privacy. A dim light helped us to see what we were doing and we agreed we would remain in bed until the other occupants of the room had left for their daily occupations. In the morning Bob suggested that perhaps we ought to try to get in a little hotel somewhere. He was thinking, of course, of Amy, and the predicament of the thing. But we felt it best not to. If we were not ready to accept their hospitality, we could hardly expect them to accept our message.

"So we remained, and that was our bedroom for three nights. Our meetings kept us up late, so we went to bed when the others in the room were asleep, and remained in bed until they moved off in the morning. What joy this family had because missionaries had come to stay with them! They were praising God because they had glass in the windows instead of cardboard, as so many had. And the one thing that amazed us most was that, before we left, the young lady purchased from us the two heaviest volumes we had—two volumes of a commentary, the most

expensive books we carried. We learned afterward that
she was going to be married to the pastor's son who was
also going to be a pastor. She bought the commentary for
his library. Our message would be forgotten, but the
books would remain. Week by week the young pastor
would be delving into the Word of God and into the
commentaries, producing messages that would be a blessing for a generation—all because we had carried books.
There is a thrill in literature work that cannot be found
in any other type of evangelism. There is a permanency
about it. When you leave, the book remains."

The goal of their journey was Vienna, then in Russian
hands. With some difficulty they received a permit to
enter though, because the Russians objected to Americans
and British accompanying each other, they had to take
different routes. Several days of meetings had been
planned, the last being arranged by the Secretary of the
Bible Society, who was delighted with their visit. He
contacted by telephone all the Christian friends he could,
and it turned out to be a meeting of fifty men, plus two
young women in their twenties. "They were conspicuous
because, other than Amy, they were the only women in
the company," said Charlton. "After the meeting, the
men made good use of the booktable before dispersing,
but the two young ladies remained behind. They were
rather timid girls and if Amy hadn't been with us, it is
unlikely they would have had the courage to approach
us at all. They explained that their train didn't leave
until eleven that night so they would help us pack up
the books. We invited them to come and eat with us.
We hadn't eaten for hours and were very hungry. But
they wouldn't eat. They would only take coffee. However,
we had an enjoyable time of fellowship together out of
which, unknown to us at the time, a great friendship
was to develop.

"The next time we were to meet was in England. They
had expressed a desire to improve their English so we

arranged for them to spend a time at our London headquarters. It was during this visit that they shared with
us the full story of that evening in Vienna. News of the
meeting had reached them by telephone just in time for
them to catch the last train for Vienna if they wished.
It was a two-hour journey. They found they had just
enough money for the return trip and no more, so they
decided to go.

"They were from a wealthy, cultured family, and had
lived in a castle home on the borders of Czechoslovakia.
During the Russian occupation the frontier had been
changed and they had lost all their property. Now they
and their aged parents were practically destitute. One
girl was a musician who had been preparing for a professional concert career in Vienna. The other had ability
with languages. Both had to drop their plans, buy a loom
and start weaving. That was why they would only take
coffee at the restaurant. They wouldn't eat because they
couldn't pay for the meal. If we had only known, how
glad we would have been to have shared with them.
They went to Vienna because they heard W.E.C. missionaries were to be there, and they had received the first
edition of *Worldwide* in German.

"After a period in England they went to a Bible college
in Germany. Now Elizabeth and Helga von Ferenchich
are missionaries of the Christian Literature Crusade in
Austria, operating a bookstore in Graz. This was one of
the thrilling outcomes of that difficult and dangerous
winter journey through the whole length of Austria. We
believe it will be permanent fruit, not only because of
the books left behind, but because these two young
women were called and used of God to establish the
work permanently in that needy country."

Jean and Marcelle Treboux from Switzerland were
the C.L.C. pioneers in France. After a survey trip from
north to south, the Lord opened the door in 1952 in the

southern village of Marguerittes, near the city of Nimes. "Living accommodation in France is something sought by many, but eventually a house was found," wrote Phil Booth in *The Silent War*. "A house? Well, yes; but what a house! The fact that the roof leaked was of little consequence in the light of its condition inside. Typical of many country towns in France, the house had then no sanitation. The previous occupants had used one of the upstairs rooms with straw on the floor. Into the back room had been swept all the rubbish of the house for many months; maybe years, for it was nearly knee-deep. Jean was staggered. Marcelle wept. The last thing they saw from their camp beds as they went to sleep the first night were large beetles climbing up the wall.

"Almost immediately Jean had to be away for a colportage tour planned months beforehand. The local rubbish-cleaning man would not look at the filth to be cleared from the new C.L.C. Headquarters. With her own hands Marcelle carried most of it to the outside of the town at night-time, and dumped it in a ditch. In the room full of rubbish she found seven rats' nests. 'Quelle joie!' she exclaimed, in telling of the experience afterwards. 'I had found something clean.'

"By sweeping some of the rubbish at the door into the pan of the collector as he ambled down the road, she won a smile from him. This, to the neighbors, was the last straw. They had been watching the lives of these strangers in their midst. There had been no barrier on account of any elegant equipment; no obvious resources different from their own; no air of supposed superiority sensed in the hearts of those around. The people saw Jesus Christ show His power in their conditions, and they wondered. But the rubbish-collector's smile opened their mouths to ask questions, and the way was open."

A friend first met Jean at a railway station. Typical of a C.L.C. pioneer he was trundling a box of literature on one of those walking sticks on wheels — his first "bookmobile."

Four years later a shop was offered by a French Christian rent-free for life, though its owner had been offered £2,000 for it by a washing machine company. Thus C.L.C. was established in northern France in the province of Brittany and in the capital city of Rennes. A third center was opened in St. Peray near Lyons, again through the offer of a rent-free shop. Two associate workers, Harvey and Yvonne Trotter from Ireland, have occupied this. In 1961 a further center was established in Nimes. The staff for all these has increased to eight by the addition of Chris Askew from Britain, Eva Mattmann from Switzerland and Paulette Bec and Huguette Teissier from France. Still others are inquiring.

France has always had the reputation of being discouraging in its reception of the gospel. It is true that anticlericalism, atheism and indifferentism on the one hand, mingled with Roman Catholicism as the religion of the large majority of those who have a faith on the other hand, make the approach to that brilliant, independent-minded, penetrating nation a double hurdle to surmount; though there are also stirrings of the Spirit here and there, and encouragements.

Charlton Smith tells of Jean Treboux selling a New Testament at the little village station of Marguerittes. It had been ordered by the station master, an unbeliever, and Jean was delivering it. "The transaction took place in front of the relief station master, whose job is to go from station to station throughout southern France, to take over during holidays or sickness. When this man saw the New Testament being given to the unbeliever, he asked, 'Where did it come from? Where can I get one?' and Jean introduced himself as the C.L.C. representative in France. This relief station master was a keen Christian. He had many links with Christians in the south of France, and mentioned in particular his own

pastor. When he learned that Jean had a Christian literature depot almost on that very railway line, he was
enthusiastic and said he would tell this good news to
other pastors. As a result about five pastors, who serve
a wide section of southern France, from the Spanish to
the Italian border, called on Jean to see his stock and
make some purchases. A later outcome was an invitation
to Jean and myself to go to Toulouse in the southwestern
part of France for a meeting.

"We arrived with our books, not knowing what to
expect. To our amazement we found that a public audi-
torium had been hired for the day. The afternoon meeting
well filled the large building. There was a freshness about
this gathering. Most of those present were very young
Christians. This was evident when we announced the
Scripture reading. There was a rustle of pages, but they
weren't familiar with the Bible and didn't know where
the books or passages were to be found. Some time had
to be given for them to find the place. Without any
embarrassment, those who could not find the place asked
help from those who could. To see such enthusiasm over
the Word of God was an inspiration in itself. In the
evening meeting there was a still larger crowd. At the
close, the people headed for the booktable with an enthusiasm very rarely seen anywhere in Britain. They
were thoughtful customers, asking about the contents of
books for their own benefit or for a relative or somebody
who wasn't a believer. 'What book do you recommend
I get for them?' was the constant inquiry. Not all the
stock was on display because the tables weren't large
enough, but French enthusiasm overflowed, and when
they saw open cartons nearby they helped themselves,
bringing the books they had chosen to the table, making
their purchases."

"Besides our book centers," says Jean, "there are about
forty people who you might call 'district representatives.'
They have booktables and occasionally do colportage and

market work. There is also an increase in orders coming from outside of France, and we now send books to Algeria, Morocco, Senegal, Ivory Coast, the Cameroons, the area formerly French West Africa, Congo Republique and French West Indies.

"Another of our tasks is collaborating with, and ministering to, the church with devotional literature, children's meetings, and evangelism. The scope is tremendous. There are at least fifty important towns of over 100,000 population with no Christian bookshop. There are thirty thousand villages and small towns where there is no vital witness for God. To meet such challenges and opportunities we are trusting the Lord for at least one hundred workers.

For a middle-aged couple with two teen-age children, a home rebuilt after having been destroyed in the war, and the husband holding a lucrative position, to become C.L.C. workers was evidently a real call of God. It cost this for Cort and Minnie Boerop of The Hague, Holland, to start the C.L.C. work in Belgium. The French population of Belgium, being more responsive, has had more gospel workers among them. The Flemish area was where the greatest need existed, and therefore the bookstore was opened in Antwerp in 1950. It was a beginning with God alone. The Boerops arrived with three shillings in their pockets. The family had nothing but bread to eat for a week. A gas stove in the corner of the one room they rented was the "kitchen"; the "dining room" was a table and three chairs; and at night the same room with divan, camp bed and floor made the "bedroom." The "booktable" was a pile of suit cases covered with a cloth; these also served as a "wardrobe."

After some months an apartment, with windows on the street level for display, was obtained near the center of the city. Soon contacts were made, but there was also opposition. A priest was standing on a chair outside the house warning the people against the Protestants—which turned out to be the best advertisement.

Yearly the sale of Bibles has increased—though small in comparison to some countries. It has been greatly helped by the R.C. Church no longer prohibiting the reading of the Scriptures. Even articles in the newspapers encourage people to read the Bible. Ignorance and prejudice are great! "A gentleman came in," reports Cort "and asked for a Bible with Isaiah in it. We showed him several Bibles and his question was: 'Is Isaiah in all of these?' We told him that every Bible has the book of Isaiah in it. His reply was: 'Oh, I didn't know that, I never have had a Bible. Once I found a part of a book called Isaiah and I have read it with interest. I want to have this book, and I have heard that it is in the Bible.'

A near neighbor, who was often unkind to them, had to be won by love. "After two and a-half years the Lord gave us an opportunity to speak with the mother. One of her remarks was: 'You cannot go to heaven, for you are Protestants.' We told her that we are not Protestants but, by grace, children of God, and we showed her that everyone can become a child of God and go to heaven through Jesus Christ alone, who died for us on the cross of Calvary. Before she went, she said: 'Yes, we see and have seen that you must all have something special.' From that time on they changed their attitude and are now very kind to us."

Much faithful work is done witnessing in the markets, and by house-to-house tract distribution in many villages. The gifts of a Volkswagen and a folding organ have greatly helped in this. When electricity in the Essen Market was refused for their public address system they were able to continue by using the battery of their car and so, nothing daunted, the work in Belgium goes on steadily.

At first the Netherlands was also served from the Antwerp base but in 1962, with the coming of a new worker, Ineke Stuiver, it was agreed that the country could be served better from a local center. A start was made in Amersfoort with colportage and mail order as the main means of distribution, but the ultimate goal will be a good store in a central location.

The help of the Spezia Mission (whose British secretary, Roland Hall, was formerly a Crusade worker), opened the door to Italy for us. Don Teall, the first to go in 1954, had the usual wait in faith for the permit, not easily obtained in the country which is the heart of Roman Catholicism. Not only was it given, but he and the three others who now have formed the C.L.C. team, Jean Henderson, Irene Stewart and Leslie Tunstell, have been able to remain and become established in the country. The first C.L.C. bookstore was opened in Florence in 1955. "At the service of dedication," writes Don, "there were pastors or representatives from all the evangelical churches in the city, and it was evident that the center was brought into being by the Lord not only as a provision for His people here, but also for those who would be afraid to enter a church. A bookshop does not resemble the place they may have been taught to shun.

"Many and varied are our visitors: local Christians, nominal Catholics, beggars, businessmen, priests and nuns. We pray that the word spoken and the tract given will bear fruit for eternity. Month after month there has been a steady increase in the volume of literature and materials going out to customers throughout the whole of Italy. Our best seller is still the Bible. Recently a priest came in and asked for a copy of the text on the wall, 'I am the Way, the Truth and the Life.' He took a Gospel of John. Another time a man came in whose attention was arrested by some of the books by Calvin, Luther, and Savanarola. A talk with him revealed a hungry heart. He told us he had bought an Italian Bible in an evangelical bookshop in Addis Ababa in 1941 and had read it during four years in a prisoner-of-war camp in Kenya. He said he would like to have more conversation with us because he felt we understood his need. When he talked with the priests they became annoyed and said he was demon-possessed. He went away with some tracts and a study course on the Gospel of John, promising to return."

Other opportunities for literature evangelism keep our workers constantly alert and on the go. For several years they had been challenged by the possibilities of stall evangelism in some of the nation's Trade Fairs. Their first opportunity came in 1962, when the city of Florence organized an International Exhibition. It was to run for just over three weeks and our workers obtained a stall in the exhibition grounds.

Their preparations included printing thousands of two specially written leaflets. One was an appeal to read the Bible; the other a good straight gospel tract entitled, *I Don't Have the Time.* Good stocks of literature were set up including two hundred Bibles which had been ordered especially for this effort. To our workers it was a veritable target of faith to see every copy sold.

The results? Beyond their highest hopes. A total of *408 Bibles,* plus New Testaments, portions and much vital literature including such titles as Billy Graham's *Peace With God.* As Don Teall said, "all sold to Catholics or atheistic unbelievers in general." Within the first week a variety of people had visited the stall and made purchases. During those days Don wrote, "Yesterday we sold *Peace With God* to a priest who was delighted to have it!" And, he continued, "Besides selling the literature we have had many precious contacts and conversations with seeking souls and interested people."

The total cost of operating this bookstall was about $250, over half of which was contributed by Italian Christians. It is encouraging to note an increasing sense of responsibility on the part of the local church to carry through its own program of gospel outreach. There are about ten large cities which run similar exhibitions and our workers believe they should push right ahead and establish a gospel literature display in each of them.

The next city to be entered with the bookstore ministry was Messina, a port of Sicily. Premises were obtained and fixtures prepared with the help of local Christians and a missionary couple from Switzerland. But the authorities were reluctant to grant a trading permit and it was turned down. Faith persisted and in the late summer of 1962 official permission was granted. Early signs indicate that this new bookstore will be an active center of ministry to the whole island.

16

NORTH AMERICA AND WORLD EXPANSION

Ken Adams paid his first visit to the U.S.A. in 1947. It was to bring to the North American fellowship a clearer understanding of the literature ministry and literature vision as God had given it to C.L.C. Britain. Up to this time, although a start had been made with a bookstore in Canada, there was no clear indication of this developing into a literature mission with a great worldwide outreach. But it did not take him long to sense the challenge of this great North American continent with all its potential for the work, in personnel, prayer and funds. Here was a land of opportunity and a people ready to respond to every challenge which would further worldwide evangelization.

"The idea of a specialized literature ministry was very new," recalls Ken, "but I believe God brought C.L.C. to North America in perfect timing. From my first visit I sensed a significant readiness in the hearts of God's people here in North America to respond to this new opportunity. I was convinced that this continent could play a sizeable part in the development of C.L.C. worldwide. And so it has proved."

Returning to England for the Annual C.L.C. Conference in 1948, Ken presented the challenge of worldwide developments and the new opportunities in North America which in turn caught the imagination of the workers, and all agreed to release Ken and Bessie Adams for the

North American program for approximately two years—
but the two years have become fifteen, and permanency!

Watching for the Lord's pattern for the C.L.C. in North
America, Ken came gradually to recognize that it might
take a form different from Britain's. At first they thought
it would be similar, and that bookstores would be opened
in the major cities of the United States and Canada.
There was already a small store in Toronto, which was
moved to better premises in a more central location, and
for two years served as the North American hub for C.L.C.
activities. About the same time a small book room was
taken over in Rochester, New York, and that also was
moved to a fine ground-floor location which greatly flour-
ished for ten years. A third bookstore was opened in
Raleigh, North Carolina, and continued for some years.
But with a clearer insight into the American scene there
came a change of ideas and policies.

"The conviction grew," says Ken, "that this type of
development was not the way of the Lord for us in North
America. Christian business people had caught the vision
of Christian bookstores, and throughout the continent
fine stores were being opened continually. We began to
see that the Lord was indicating some other lines of
emphasis for us, which have subsequently developed into
two major ministries. First, we noticed that there were
certain types of 'deeper life' books missing from the
catalogs of North American publishers. With our knowledge of the British Christian book world, we felt that we
should introduce some of these titles to the North American reading public. From this there developed what we
call the British book program—which would include books
by such authors as Oswald Chambers, Andrew Murray,
Jessie Penn-Lewis, Amy Carmichael, Watchman Nee (*The
Normal Christian Life*), Roy Hession (*The Calvary Road*),
and others. The British home front was again ready to
make a practical contribution to worldwide expansion,

and gave North America two of their best workers in this field of mail order development—Leslie and Nora Fitton.

"The other significant conviction was that North America should become a strong sending home base. We felt we should concentrate on the overseas expansion and make a concerted effort to help meet the growing world-wide need for Christian literature. The call for help was reaching us continually. For us this meant seeing the Lord provide personnel and adequate supporting finances, not only for the workers but also for the actual job of establishing bookstores with all the necessary fixtures and fittings and an adequate supply of stock. Then as the work became established there would be the need for national expansion—other bookstores, mobile units, publishing in the national or major languages and so on. To His praise we can testify that this aspect of the work has expanded steadily over the years and we believe the next few years are going to see further sizeable advances.

"By our twenty-first year (1962) the Crusade operates in thirty-six countries. Five of these are what we call home base countries: United States, Canada, United Kingdom, Australia and New Zealand. Of the remaining thirty-one overseas areas, North America is responsible for twenty-two, Great Britain for eight, and Australia for one. This, I think, indicates that what we had believed was the Lord's pattern for the work in North America has been amply proven to be so. Without exception, every country entered has been at the direct invitation of, or in response to, constant appeals from people concerned for their country.

"The first real emphasis on world outreach came at the end of World War II. It was not until 1946 that we were able to make any serious moves into other parts of the world because of restrictions on travel. At the same time several things began fitting together to bring the challenge of literature into sharper focus. One was the fact that Dr. Frank Laubach had launched into his great

Dedication Day, September 23, 1961, drew a crowd of interested friends.

The dedication service held in the main office area.

One section of the general office.

Typesetting in the North American print shop.

The printer — a vital person.

Bookkeeping — another key function.

Keeping the Mail Order Department running smoothly.

Two views of the new print shop in the North American
headquarters.

The Paramatta book-shop, near Sydney, Australia.

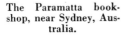

Inside the Paramatta shop.

Ample stocks in the Montreal bookstore, Quebec, Canada.

George daCosta, co-director
in the West Indies.

Donald David, C.L.C.
field leader in India.

Jose and Norma Wojnarowicz,
Argentina, South America.

Mr. & Mrs. Jean Treboux,
pioneers in France.

Kawai-san and family, Japan.

Left to Right: Solomon Balinbin,
Narciso Palomar, Ben Naguit, Floro
Matunog, print-shop team in the
Philippines.

Working on the plans for the *Caribbean Challenge* magazine in the Kingston, Jamaica office.

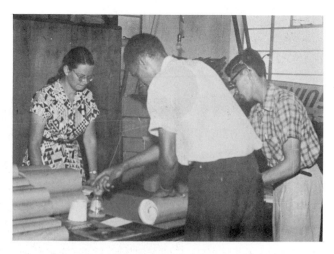

The first issues of *Challenge* being prepared for inter-island distribution.

Thelma Cooper edits
the material.

Marion Manning pro-
cesses the business.

Julaine Smith prepares the
art.

Grace Chang assists two Chinese customers in the Surabaja, Java center.

Willard Stone and an Indonesian customer in the Surabaja store.

Satisfied customers conclude their purchases in the center in Tokyo, Japan.

An attractive booktable in Japan draws eager young customers.

Japan Field Conference—1961.

Maurice Thomas takes the books to a crowded market
in New Guinea.

Above: The Madras, India bookstore.

Right: One section of the Ambassador Book Store in downtown Madras.

Interior of the Mussoorie, India C.L.C. center.

Above: The attractive center in Bangkok, Thailand

Above: Porto Alegre, Brazil exhibits eye-catching displays.

Right: A corner of the bookstore in Santiago, Chile.

Expansion in Monrovia, Liberia, West Africa—
new premises occupied in November 1962.

Right: Interior of
the Bissau Chris-
tian Bookshop in
Portuguese Guinea,
West Africa.

Below: The C.L.C.
print shop in the
Philippines.

The British mail order department moved to this new building in 1969.

At the dedication of the new facilities a group enjoys a sampling of the books in the warehouse.

Forced to relocate by a new highway the C.L.C. in Australia put up
these new headquarters buildings in 1969.

In 1965, C.L.C. North America moved into these new housing units.

campaign of world literacy. His simplified methods of teaching and learning were being received enthusiastically by governments throughout the world. This in itself indicated to us clearly that governments were determined to improve education in their countries. It seemed as though the leadership of the world had suddenly become aware of the bottle-neck to national and international progress—the ignorance of the common people. But even before this drive for literacy brought its new challenge, we in C.L.C. had been aroused to the fact that there were areas of the world with English as the national language where no serious attempt had yet been made to supply English literature, even though usually there was a higher percentage of literacy in such countries. We also discovered that with the growing drive for education around the world, young people were showing an increasing desire to learn English, which they recognized to be the international language. Therefore we noted with interest that even in non - English - speaking countries, such as Japan and Indonesia, there were open doors for English Christian literature.

"Added to this, there is the exploding population of the world. We are told that within the next forty years the present three billion population will more than double. This means that the second three billion will be under forty years of age. Even now this youthful aspect of the world is upon us. Brazil, for instance, claims that 50 per cent of its population is twenty-one years and under. So we have ahead of us a young world, eagerly learning, many having at least an elementary education. We believe it is tremendously important to get literature into the hands of this mass of young people—literature that will introduce them to Christ and lead them on in the ways of righteousness.

"A further constant challenge has been the tremendous activity of the cults, and the ever-increasing advance of Communism. These use the printed page extensively in what could well be called "printed-page evangelism.' They have gone about the job with missionary zeal and real sacrifice. The type of literature they put out offers plenty of quantity and quality for a very nominal sum so that all who will can buy freely. We in evangelical circles could learn much from the methods and techniques such groups employ.

"In the early days of C.L.C. history we felt very much alone in this field of literature evangelism. It seemed as though we were a voice crying in the wilderness while others were busy with different aspects of the missionary program. But praise God over these past ten years there has been growing evidence of a tremendous increase of interest on the part of God's people in this type of missionary work. Consequently, the output of Christian literature around the world has greatly increased.

"I had always felt that in North America the challenge of literature should be presented to the Christian public by an independent organization that could draw the missions together in their respective literature ministries. Through the *Floodtide* magazine and other publicity the Lord was beginning to bring C.L.C. into a place of recognition as a literature organization, yet in the thinking of many it was just another mission and did not command any place of special significance. It could never become the literature 'voice' to the Christian public in a truly inter-mission sense. But such a 'voice' was soon to be heard. Clyde Taylor, Executive Secretary of the Evangelical Foreign Missions Association, had been showing a growing and sympathetic interest in our program. On one occasion I spent the night in the Taylors' home and shared with him some of the wider burdens on my heart, particularly this thought of a group bringing the challenge of literature to the nation as a whole. My feeling was that perhaps he was the man who could bring such a thing into being because of his link with the National Association of Evangelicals. He was extremely interested,

and the ultimate outcome of our talk was a special conference exclusively to discuss the need for literature
representation on a nation-wide and world-wide scale.
Springing out of this conference a five-man committee
was set up to study the subject more closely. The result
was the formation, in 1952, of Evangelical Literature
Overseas which, under the able leadership of Harold
Street as Executive Secretary, has been recognized and
accepted as an interdenominational, inter-mission literature organization. I am convinced that this has been one
of the most significant developments in the expansion of
the literature ministry.

"A second suggestion I shared with Clyde Taylor that
evening was the hope that one day there would be in
North America, and perhaps eventually around the world,
a Sunday set aside as World Literature Sunday. It was
thought that on this particular day sermons and Sunday
School lessons could be focused on the need of missionary
literature in the world. As a Board member of E.L.O.,
I later shared this suggestion with the committee. It was
accepted and for the past five years World Literature
Sunday has been a regular feature each second Sunday
in October, organized under the sponsorship of Evangelical Literature Overseas.

"Other groups also have greatly increased their literature emphasis, in particular the Moody Press and Colportage Department. A few years ago, as an indication of
their growing concern for world literature, they changed
their name to Moody Literature Mission, and have
consistently given practical help to worthwhile literature
projects. Then the Back to the Bible Broadcast of Lin-
coln, Nebraska, under the leadership of Theodore Epp
and G. Christian Weiss, have very appreciably stepped
up their interest in national and world literature and
continue to make a very significant contribution to missionary literature projects. Christian Life Missions, founded and led by Rev. Carl Tanis, is another agency which

has made literature its major emphasis and contributed considerably to the opening of bookstores, the purchasing of mobile units and the publishing of literature and gospel magazines. In each case these groups have helped our own C.L.C. program in no small way, and we are deeply grateful to them.

"Several other fine literature groups have come into being and are making a very real contribution in mass tract and booklet distribution. Then older established organizations, such as the Pocket Testament League, have stepped up their production and distribution most significantly since the end of the war. Of course the great Bible societies push steadily forward in their prime ministry of making available the Word of God in the language of the people. Working closely in this field are the 800 or so missionaries of the Wycliffe Bible Translators who press toward their goal of putting some portion of Scripture into the more than 2,000 as yet unwritten languages.

"In my travels around the world, I have been much encouraged to see the greatly expanded literature ministry of some of the missions. I think particularly of the splendid work of the Word of Life Press associated with The Evangelical Alliance Mission, especially in Japan; and the ministry of the Christian Witness Press in Hongkong, under the auspices of the China Inland Mission, and which is spreading to other areas such as the Philippines. Bible correspondence courses, such as those of the Source of Light Mission and World Gospel Crusades, have mostly come into being during the 1950's and been tremendously used of the Lord in bringing the Gospel and God's Word to the people.

The first popular-type magazine, *African Challenge*, made its debut in July 1951 with a modest 5,000 copies. Today its monthly edition averages 150,000, and in its train a dozen other such papers have come into being including our own *Caribbean Challenge*.

On my visit to Europe in 1961 I was greatly thrilled

to see so much good literature going out. I met some enthusiastic literature workers in unlikely places. Much of this European work was the direct result of young, American-born George Verwer, whose yearly 'Operation Mobilization' is saturating country after country with vital Christian literature. His fellow workers are largely students who give a couple of months of their summer vacation to this literature work. As a result of the 1962 campaign more than 20,000 people made personal application for a correspondence course or similar piece of literature.

"Another significant development has been the start of Literature Fellowships around the world, largely under the inspiration of Evangelical Literature Overseas. I was present with John Davey and George daCosta in Costa Rica at the birth of L.E.A.L., the literature fellowship for Spanish South America: Brazil has its C.L.E.B., India its E.L.F.I., and so on around the world. There are possibly fifteen or twenty of these literature fellowships representative of all the missions working in the specific countries or language areas. One of the most valuable contributions these fellowships make is the running of literature workshops in key areas, where national Christians are given instruction in the ways and means of operating a Christian bookstore, doing colportage work, or tackling journalism and editorial work."

17

RISE UP AND BUILD

The finding of Camp Hill, Fort Washington, Pennsylvania, and the establishing of W.E.C.-C.L.C. Headquarters in North America was another romance of faith. At first the Crusade had shared headquarters in Chicago. Then, to give them more elbowroom, the C.L.C. moved from Chicago and occupied the W.E.C. Headquarters on Germantown Avenue, Philadelphia. Soon these also proved inadequate and there came a growing conviction that we should look to God for a combined headquarters large enough to house both Crusades, and for expansion. An intensified search brought to Ken's attention a property located in Fort Washington, Pa. consisting of sixty-seven acres of woodland. This place, known as Camp Hill, is of historical significance because George Washington had stationed some of his troops there during the Revolutionary War prior to moving to Valley Forge. In 1882 one of the wealthy families of Philadelphia built a summer home there. It consisted of the main building —a large stone mansion of about forty rooms constructed to resemble a Scottish castle—a tall and stately water tower, coach houses, stables and other buildings, all made of the same massive stonework. Both hill and mansion are landmarks in the surrounding country, overlooking the broad Whitemarsh Valley to the Germantown ridge of Philadelphia, five miles distant.

Ken, along with others, went to inspect the property. "We went to look at the place on Thanksgiving afternoon

1951," he remembers. "It certainly was a mess. The majority felt convinced that this place was unsuitable, so serious was the damage caused by vandalism. My reaction was more favorable. I went through every room, including the dark and dismal basement which stretched from one end of the large house to the other. Then as I looked across the grounds and saw the other stone buildings (about six in all) I felt there were 'possibilities' here in spite of the poor condition of the buildings. We made inquiry through the real estate agent and found that the asking price was $150,000 for twenty-four acres and the buildings! That seemed to be the end of that."

In a neighboring district is a remarkable work of faith called Christ's Home, where difficult children are entrusted by the authorities to the care and education by its devoted workers. They are wholly a work of faith, members of a German-American community whose deep roots reach back to the piety and spirituality of those same communities in their Fatherland. Many generous gifts of furnishings and produce have been shared with the Crusade from time to time by these dear friends as God has prospered them. Shortly after this visit of inspection to Camp Hill, one of the C.L.C. workers spent a weekend at Christ's Home and, in course of conversation, learned that the owner of Camp Hill was known to several. A contact was made, and the owner expressed much interest when she found that the Crusade operated on a similar basis of faith. Because the property was so damaged through vandalism and had been empty for two years, she reduced the price considerably for all the buildings and twenty-four acres. Instead, we boldly asked her for the whole sixty-seven acres, with the thought of selling off some of the land. "I asked what her rock-bottom price would be," says Ken. "After a moment of thought she made a remarkable offer. 'You are doing a good work,' she said, 'and as it is like Christ's Home to which I feel very attracted, I will let you have everything for $65,000.'

I could hardly believe my ears and am sure I must have revealed my surprise by the look on my face! Remarkable and generous as this offer was this was still a fantastic sum for a missionary society and I knew we did not have any money. Yet I was very sure God was leading. In my heart I had a feeling that we might well be on the threshold of another demonstration of the faithfulness of our God. That it was indeed a miracle-in-the-making we were soon to see.

"I felt the only course open to me was to give the full picture even though I was acutely aware of how foolish it must have sounded. But that was good for my pride, and having gone thus far I had no intention of turning back. In a nutshell these were the facts I presented. We could make an immediate cash down payment of $2,000. The mission would sell its two houses in Chicago and Philadelphia. After prior commitments these might produce, say $20,000. I had no immediate solution to offer regarding the remaining funds which would be needed. She was evidently impressed and voluntarily offered to arrange a $40,000 mortgage at a reasonable interest.

"Armed with these facts I went to our Chicago Headquarters and shared the full story with the staff, including the details regarding the very bad condition of the buildings. The result was that two of the brethren Alfred Ruscoe and Bob Butters, returned with me to look the place over. Snow had fallen quite heavily and a group of us trudged up the hillside wondering what lay ahead. Fog and sleet made it about as inauspicious a day as there could be for such an assignment. But again the Lord witnessed to our hearts that He was leading. Mr. Ruscoe's comment was almost identical to my own first impressions —'It's got possibilities.' Finally we agreed to move forward and were ready to talk to the owner about the proposed purchase. She came down in price yet another $5,000. We agreed to buy the place for $60,000 and, to clinch the deal, made a $2,000 down payment on Christmas Eve 1951.

"The day of final settlement came early in 1952. Neither house had yet been sold so we were still without the necessary funds to consumate the transaction. What were we to do? Confidently we went to the real estate office to 'sign on the dotted line.' Here I was informed that at this time the fee of $3,000 had to be paid as part of the usual settlement practices. I had neither check nor cash in my possession! It was a ticklish moment for, after all, here we were purporting to be fully ready to buy this sizeable piece of real estate. But deliverance was at hand. A brief review of the situation with the owner settled it and she promptly wrote out a check for this full amount. Seeing we had only made a nominal down payment of $2,000 it actually cost her $1,000 to let the Crusade take over Camp Hill! To us it was yet another evidence of the greatness of our God, touching the heart of this comparative stranger and using her to fulfill His greater purposes." The two houses were sold a few months later and a further $18,000 paid, leaving just the mortgage outstanding.

The job of repair and renovation had been started as soon as the initial agreement to purchase had been made. It was a monumental job. There were about 400 window panes to be replaced, just to mention one item. All the work was done by the staff and candidates, assisted by outside friends who gave gladly of their time and technical skills of plumbing, carpentry, paper hanging, painting and so on. Gradually all the buildings were put into usable order; some became offices, some were turned into the Mail Order Department and warehouse. The stables were converted into a print shop. Soon every nook and cranny of the large mansion (besides other buildings which were transformed into living quarters) was filled with personnel—staff, candidates and missionaries on furlough, usually a 'family' of about sixty adults and twenty-five children. How thankful we were that God had guided to such an estate with such possibilities of expansion.

"As far as C.L.C. was concerned," continues Ken, "we anticipated steady development in the work which would necessitate more living quarters and a more adequate building for a print shop, mail order program and general offices. Several years went by, and we had our hands full keeping the current program operating as well as working on the general repairs of the existing buildings. Then in 1956 we began to face the necessity of building further accommodations for the C.L.C. personnel. Here again God worked in a wonderful way.

"Two significant things had happened which helped clear the way for such expansion. We had been compelled to sell a small portion of the land to the highway authorities for the construction of a new expressway from north Philadelphia. As a result we were able to reduce our mortgage considerably. Then the highway contractors needed a lot of earth for fill and asked if we would sell some from our hillside. The money from this further transaction together with two earmarked gifts from friends of the Crusade, enabled the entire mortgage to be wiped out. Needless to say there was much rejoicing. Faith had leaped another hurdle and the miracle of Camp Hill was complete. Remarkably also this excavation for the earth resulted in a large flat area on a level with the new Expressway which, in due course, would prove admirably suitable as a location for the C.L.C. administrative offices, print shop and warehouse. Now we could look forward in faith to the day when such a building would be put up. However, the immediate need was for housing for our personnel, and the Lord has wonderfully enabled for three buildings to be completed as a start.

"But faith still looked forward to the administration building on the excavated land. There we would be easily accessible from the new Expressway, and also would be seen from the Pennsylvania Turnpike which runs close by. But the more we learned about building, the more we realized that there were big costs involved, and it looked to us as though the day was far distant when we could begin such an extensive building program. Then one day a wonderful thing happened. The phone rang and a voice on the other end asked, 'Is this Mr. Adams? Well, I would like to have a little talk with you, as I understand you are doing some building on Camp Hill.'

" 'Yes,' I replied, 'we are busy putting up some homes for the workers. God is extending the ministry of the Crusade, and we need more room.'

" 'That is interesting,' he answered. 'But what about your office and print-shop building?'

" 'Well, we do have some rather tentative plans,' I said, 'but nothing very definite. A building like that is going to cost quite a bit of money.'

" 'Well,' said this friend, 'would you seriously contemplate going ahead if you had some money?' "

The end of that conversation was an off-hand estimate by Ken that it would cost at least $50,000 and a statement by 'the voice' that he would try to provide between $30,000 and $40,000 if C.L.C. could find the rest. 'The voice' refused to identify himself, and Ken said, "This is almost too good to be true. It seems as though I must be talking to an angel in heaven.

" 'I don't think you are,' the answer came, 'but if we can help in some way, we would like to.' "

Ken consulted with his staff, and when the friend called again three days later, the answer was ready; Yes, they would go forward. A few weeks afterward came a check for $35,000. "To this day we don't know the name or whereabouts of this good gentleman," says Ken.

The costs turned out to be more than the estimate. After talks with an architect and estimates from several builders it was evident the final price would be around $60,000. Then a new road had to be cut because the Expressway was a limited-access highway, so the total cost was nearer $80,000. However, the builder, a keen Christian, was willing to go ahead on the basis of a split contract, spending up to the amount available on the shell of the building. "But somehow we felt sure the Lord would never let us put up a shell," says Ken, "and then let it stand for a couple of years unused. But faith always has to go just one step at a time.

"The actual construction began a few weeks before I was to leave for a visit to Europe in the spring of 1961. Now we were truly involved and had to face the issue of the future in reality. What was the Lord leading us to do? Were we to go just as far as the roof and then leave it, or what? We had several prayer meetings. In one of these one of the candidates prayed, 'Lord, you have really got us out on the limb now, why don't You saw the limb off and let us fall into the everlasting arms underneath?!' That brought the laugh of faith from us as our hearts responded. That was a tremendous prayer meeting and at our business meeting a few days later it was fairly easy to recognize that the Lord's will for us was to move forward. We would tell the contractor to go right ahead and complete the building. With this clear word of the Lord in our hearts we knew that the funds would be in hand to meet each bill as it fell due. One further word which the Lord had made clear to us was that this building was to be a faith project in the strictest sense of the word, and we were not to raise a finger to borrow funds through the regular channels of a bank mortgage. Neither were we to touch mission funds; that is, the gifts that God's people send to help forward the work around the world. We were just to watch Him provide for us.

"Soon after I left for Europe the news came that we had spent all our money. The $35,000 was completely gone and we were overdrawn by a few hundred dollars. What were we to do? We had committed ourselves, and the builder had already proceeded with his plans. Faith was being tested, but God was working. It was a happy day

shortly after when I received a brief letter from Reg Fife,
who was acting as deputy leader, saying, 'Hallelujah,
$25,000 for the building program.' I don't know if he
heard my 'Hallelujah' from the other side of the Atlantic!

"The building proceeded apace so that we were able to
have our official opening and dedication on September
23, 1961. What a joy it was to be able to state that every
bill which had been presented had been paid, and we
didn't owe anybody anything. Of course there were other
bills to come and unfinished work to be done. Before
long the money was gone again and once more we entered
into the real battle of faith. We called several more
prayer meetings and watched to see what God would do.
He did respond but not in the way we had expected.
Again I was called to the telephone. A close friend of the
work who was watching and praying with us wanted me
to know that he and his wife had some funds lying idle.
This money could not be given outright as it was to be
used for another purpose, but we could use it in the
meantime, and it would be interest free. So a further
$10,000 came. This caused some deep heart-searching.
Frankly we wanted to see the Lord send us another gift,
yet we had to acknowledge that this was the Lord's
wonderful and timely provision for the present. We had
not asked anyone; the suggestion had come without any
seeking on our part. There were still more bills to be met,
but the Lord gave us such a successful Christmas season
we were able to use some of our own funds to meet these.
Other gifts also came in so that on March 16, 1962 the
last bill was paid, thus completing a project of almost
$80,000 in less than one year from the time the founda-
tions were laid. So God literally provided step by step in
this the largest single adventure of faith in Crusade
history.

"But the story doesn't stop there. Although outwardly
this building was very attractive and we were certainly
happy with it, inside we had only the bare essentials.

Much was still needed to make things attractive and efficient—packing benches, shelves, furnishings, fittings and office equipment. In our prayer room we had a medley of chairs, worn and tattered, a bit out of place in such a nice room. We were content with them, though in the back of our minds we wondered if some day the Lord would enable us to get chairs more in keeping with this lovely room. Then things began to happen. Some comfortable arm chairs were sent in which proved suitable for the reception lobby and some offices. Next the Lord sent along another friend who was in the construction business. He has made a wonderful contribution in shelving, benches and furnishings, each of which has truly 'beautified the house of the Lord.' One day he came and talked about chairs for the prayer room and then indicated that he and his wife would like to make a contribution of two dozen chairs. So today we have these beautiful chairs which tone in with the room itself.

"We hadn't been open more than a week when another friend and his wife came to see me. He was a gardener, now retired, but keeping on with some gardening as a hobby. 'You have a lot of ground around this building,' he said, 'and I think that it would look nice if you had some shrubs and evergreens. Would you object if I brought along one or two bushes?' That same afternoon he was around with a load or two of top soil. Within a week he had the grounds in front of the building looking trim and spruce with a fine display of plants and bushes. How we rejoice in the loving-kindness of the Lord, even in ways like this."

Twenty-one years ago there was just one little upstairs bookroom in a provincial town in England started with a borrowed £100. Today the work sprawls across the world into thirty-six countries and on every continent. The program is carried on through more than seventy book centers. A score of mobile units travel the highways. Publishing, from simple tracts to an 800-page concordance, is carried on in many languages. Distribution in a variety of ways now exceeds one million dollars annually, and property values climb toward the half-million mark. And of the hundreds of souls saved and lives blessed through the ministry there is no telling. What hath God wrought! We stand aside to declare unequivocally that this is the Lord's doings and it is marvelous in our eyes.

18

FUNCTIONING BY FAITH

The team of C.L.C. workers in each home base is really God's day-to-day miracle more than any material supply; hours of work given daily to the Lord without remuneration, extending to months, years and a lifetime, is a daily miracle in a self-loving, self-seeking world. Just as big a miracle is when we humans, each ourselves, each different from anyone else, each with our obvious weaknesses as well as strengths, can live in the closeness of a communal life and love one another. That is no static automatic relationship—once achieved and never again disturbed. No indeed. Brotherly love is a daily walk, a daily adventure. Personalities are meant to differ. That makes the wheels of life and progress go round. Each has different gifts, different characteristics, different outlooks. The interflow and interaction of a team in fellowship is the manifestation of Christ in His body. It is the outgoing of Christ to the world, drawing all men by the attractiveness of people loving one another which, as the apostle John says, is God dwelling in them. Such an interlove is neither gained nor maintained easily. The appeals of the Apostle Paul to "be of the same mind" to those with whom he was in most intimate spiritual rapport of all the churches—the Philippians—demonstrate that. There never will be a fellowship in perfect love on earth without a weak link in the chain; but a standard of spontaneous fellowship can be a fact. This is of another dimension than what the world can know, for we can see and reckon

on Christ in each other; and we know our own human
frailties enough to accept our brother with his idiosyn-
crasies, even as we ask him to accept us. We can have
faith that Christ in him will conform him to His image,
even as He is in the process of conforming us; and we
can healthily recognize and accept the variety of view-
points and diversity of gifts which by God's endowment
makes the many members of the one body.

There is a saying in W.E.C.—half serious, half joking—
that "the woman is the man to do it" where there have
been instances on fields of a woman doing a man's job;
and the same can be said of C.L.C. Anyhow it can certainly be said about the printshop at Fort Washington.
It is amazing to see all the variety of presses and their
accessories in heavy machinery, and to realize that all this
is handled by one young woman, right through all the
printing processes of book and magazine publishing, and
to see the list of publications, large and small. She has
had help because most of the home base workers have
given a hand at one time or another, and there has been
voluntary help by those we call "overtimers"; but Virginia
Walton is *the* printer. Her testimony sheds a lot of light
into the making of a Crusader.

"I was at Westmont College in Santa Barbara, California," she writes, "when, at a W.E.C. conference meeting, Ken Adams spoke and I knew immediately in my
heart that 'this was it.' I have never doubted since then
that C.L.C. was my calling. There have been many
times, when the going has been rough and the Holy Spirit
was dealing with me, that I've wanted to run. I doubt
if there is one in C.L.C. today who hasn't had that
'wanting-to-run' experience—but the call was so real that
if I did run, I knew it would be in direct disobedience
to Him. I wouldn't trade the rough times for anything,
as He manifested Himself over and over again to my
heart when I've yielded to Him.

"Even during school years He was guiding. While I

was in high school a friend who had a mimeograph shop offered to teach me the mimeograph and other machines. This was the beginning of my love for and my 'ability' with machinery. I also learned to operate the Varityper at that time. Because of my interest in machinery I took a course in Duplicating Processes and Business Machines in school. I was exposed to many kinds of processes including the offset printing method, having no idea that later it would be used in His program. In these ways the Lord was preparing and put it in my heart (although again I didn't recognize it as being the Lord) to operate a Christian print shop. It never occurred to me that there was that type of work within missionary circles. After high school I enlisted in the navy. On my discharge I decided to go to Westmont College and there the Lord got hold of me in a *real* way (I had been saved several years before) and I fully consecrated my life to Him for His service.

"Though acquainted with W.E.C., the Lord never seemed to quicken me about specific missionary service until the conference when Ken spoke on literature and touched on various phases of the ministry. I knew then beyond a shadow of a doubt that this was for me. I saw for the first time the need for behind-the-scenes missionaries. I couldn't picture myself behind a book counter, but I was willing to do whatever the Lord wanted. So I applied to the Crusade and listed all my 'qualifications' as far as machinery and things I could do. Ken's reply has always stuck in my heart: 'I am delighted to know of your interest in the C.L.C. ministry and your sense of call to such work. We, on our side, have been asking the Lord to bring into our ranks qualified personnel in such practical things as you outline. But I would urge you to consider carefully the fact that it is not our qualifications that matter. The Lord needs just "us," qualifications or no, for if we come into any work because of "qualifications" it is more than likely we'll not make the grade. In the final analysis these things will not keep us in the ministry to which we set ourselves—the devil will see to that. Only as you are sure of *Him* and know that you serve *Him* alone, and that all your wisdom and strength day by day comes from *Him,* will you be able to keep "steadfast and unmovable." '

"So in 1954 I came into the work. When I arrived I found a print shop with almost no workers and a backlog of work. There were three or four foreign manuscripts to be typeset and printed which had been on hand for almost two years. The equipment consisted of two Multilith presses (a small and larger model), a manually-operated cutter and a long-past-repair folder held together with wire, banding tape and what-have-you. The camera was old but with the proper 'know-how' put out good work. My heart was immediately drawn out to this phase of the ministry and I knew that this was His place for me. However, the Lord had a very basic work to do in me (as I suppose He has with all new candidates) —to let Him take over in my life instead of my helping Him out.

"I was first assigned to the task of housecleaning and any extra time I had could be spent in the print shop. Seeing the need in the print shop and my 'qualifications' for that, I didn't see why others couldn't do the housecleaning. Surely there was something wrong in the distribution of 'qualified' personnel. I stewed over this for some time and when I got to the point of desperation, He showed me that He didn't want my *service for* Him but my *fellowship with* Him, and was I going to work *for* Him or *with* Him? Wasn't it for Him to work *through* me in any way He saw fit. Was I willing for it? When I yielded to Him the work became a joy and I was ready to stay on housecleaning the rest of my days if He wanted it that way.

"One of the first jobs I helped Ken print was *The Cal-vary Road.* Because of shortage of personnel Ken was doing the printing in his 'spare time.' He was pushing through on this job as he had to leave for meetings the next morning. It took about three hours to print one plate and we had finished a plate about midnight. 'All right now,' he said, 'let's go on with the next one.' I questioned the hour but put the plate on the presss and continued to work, a little rebellious in my spirit. The title of the chapter we were printing was, 'Are you Willing to be a Servant?' and as copy after copy came off the press, this stood out. The Lord really spoke to my heart through this, as He has done with many other jobs since as they have come off the press."

As Virginia settled into the print shop work God sent new equipment in various ways; folder, cutter, presses, platemaking machine and camera. Meanwhile those from the W.E.C. staff who had been helping, Evie Schoettler and Elwin Palmer, had to return to their own jobs. This left Virginia and another young woman, Bonnie Hanson as the only regular workers in the print shop.

"Bonnie took over the photography," continued Virginia, "and was also doing all the art work, displays and designing, as well as editing *Floodtide*. This left me with the typesetting, layout, all the print shop machinery to operate, as well as the bindery. We never had a dull moment as we learned together, both being so inexperienced. We also had the help of many 'overtimers' (Christian friends and young people's groups) who would come up and give us many hours at night in the bindery.

"Several people asked how I could manage such heavy work but all the praise and glory goes to the Lord. I have found over and over again that He never gives us anything to do beyond what He enables, in strength as well as wisdom. One glimpse of His guiding hand in my early training was that at Westmont, 'for fun,' I took instruction in weight lifting. I learned how to lift heavy weights with the least amount of effort and thus avoid muscle strain. I have found this invaluable.

"There was plenty of opportunity, literally, to come to

the end of my own physical endurance. At one time we had committed ourselves to a lot of work on the strength of an experienced printer coming into the Crusade. This new worker didn't make the grade but we still had the work and the deadlines to be met. Ken was away on meetings and I was the only person who could 'solve' the situation. We soon realized we weren't going to meet the deadlines as the press would only go so fast, so the only thing was to run the presses longer, which meant more hours. I began early in the morning, keeping the presses running until late at night almost non-stop. My meals were brought out to me and I ate them while the presses were running. For three and one-half months I was putting in fifteen and sixteen hours a day, six days a week. I soon came to the end of my own strength. At night I would be exhausted and in the mornings I could hardly get up; but when I did, I felt His strength taking over. By the time I started working I was 'raring' to go, getting stronger and more refreshed as the hours went on until I finished the day's work. I found that while I was on the job I had all the strength I needed. Afterwards when I didn't need it, I didn't have it, but He always gave a good night's rest. The joy of the Lord became my strength in marvelous ways when the presses had to keep rolling sometimes in spite of illness and other physical infirmities.

"Most of my learning was through the trial-and-error method. Quite often I ran into things I just didn't know how to handle. I put all my 'knowledge' to work and tried figuring things out to find the trouble. Being mechanically inclined helped a lot, but even then I found I didn't know much. Then I began to grow into the reality of this truth—that He could be and *was* our wisdom. I gradually experienced His taking over in problems; He would center my human understanding in a certain area until I would notice the trouble. This happened over and over again. Once while on the big press the paper wasn't feeding in properly. I tried to reason this out for two days and was getting desperate. Then He centered my thoughts on a different theory from the one I was working on, and directed my attention to a certain area where I noticed a broken part, a part I never even knew existed. When I would take the press apart to repair something I would just remember where everything went. On one occasion with the folder I removed a part and all of the gears fell out of this one section. I had no idea where they went or how they fitted together. He enabled me to get them all back again—like fitting together a jig-saw puzzle.

"This one particular time on the folder was a highlight in my experience of Him revealing His wisdom to me. I worked and reasoned on this problem for two days. The third day I was really desperate. I thought I would call the folder company, as they would often give advice over the phone, but I found the phone was out of order that day. I was really at the end of all *human* help. I went to my room in utter defeat, and cried out and poured my heart out to the Lord. After a spell of self-pity I fixed my eyes on the Lord instead of on myself and my troubles. Receiving His rest in my heart, I waited quietly before Him. At that moment, He brought to my remembrance a Navy handbook we had with instructions for our particular make and model of folder. It seemed as if a great light had dawned and I just *knew* that the answer was in that book somewhere. It's hard to explain the feeling I had—it was one of those things that was so real. I literally ran back to the print shop, found the book, and He not only showed me in words, but by three pictures, to make sure I could solve the problem!

"The print shop ministry isn't always a behind-the-scenes job. Often we have opportunities to witness to salesmen. A good point of contact usually develops when they find out the 'exceptional' work we do with so little know-how. I've shown samples of certain jobs to the

Multilith salesman and he would scratch his head in bewilderment and disbelief—those jobs just couldn't have been done on our particular type of Multilith as it was 'impossible'! Our ignorance and lack of experience often opened opportunities to testify to the Lord's abundant enabling—'The foolish . . . shall confound the wise.'

"I feel the program, as it stands today, is on the threshold of blossoming out into greater fulfillment of its original vision. Because of the increased space and more adequate facilities provided by our new building, we are looking to the Lord for an experienced offset printer. My own personal burden is to see more foreign typesetting and printing done. The cry from the missionaries is for their translations to be published in the shortest possible time. We want to be in the place always of being able to help out when these needs arise, doing such printing here in the States as is practicable.

"It has been a thrill to my heart to realize the worldwide impact of this print shop ministry. One week we've been ministering to Africans and another to the Spanish-speaking areas of the world. At one time three different languages were being worked on at the same time in various phases of production. No one 'regular' missionary could ever do that! It is a thrill to realize as a foreign job is being printed that it is the Bread of Life to feed hungry souls."

C.L.C. also seems to go in for women editors — in Britain, West Indies and North America! Bonnie Hanson trained for a short period in an art school where the witness of the Inter-varsity Christian Fellowship set her on her feet for Christ. Then, while at the Bethany Fellowship, Minneapolis (from which W.E.C. and C.L.C. have received so many recruits) she heard Ken Adams speak on particular spheres of service in C.L.C. which were right along her line of interest. Following this, was a call from God "so definite and so wonderful to my heart" she says, "that it is more clear to me than my

actual salvation." It needs to be as certain as that, for
this is the very thing that will hold you in the storms.

"Coming into the work full-time, I had my battles,"
continues Bonnie. "When I first came I prayed that the
Lord would mature me, and my, what 'storms' came after
that! But storms mature us. They drive our roots deeper
and we learn to cling to God. Along with that the Lord
gives us a generous dose of disillusionment with our co-
workers, the people over us in the Lord, the mission and
everything, until we are thoroughly cast on Him. Then
we're safe because it's just us, the Lord and our commission. That's the way it should be and that's what He
wants!

"It was during my first year in the mission that the
Lord spoke to me definitely about taking up the magazine
work. This was quite a strange thing in the natural,
because I had neither the qualifications for editorial work
nor the proper training for art. So I can only say that
the Lord 'chooses the foolish things' with which to do
His work.

"When I began on my first issue of *Floodtide* I realized
how far in 'over my head' I was, and how little I knew
of what I was supposed to be doing. At that time I was
reading consecutively in Exodus. The Lord gave me a
word of encouragement and spoke it so forcefully to my
heart that it has been with me ever since. It is found in
the story where the Lord was calling out the workers for
the tabernacle and reads, 'And the Lord spoke unto Moses,
saying, See, I have called by name Bezaleel . . . and I have
filled him with the spirit of God, in wisdom, and in
understanding, and in knowledge, and in all manner of
workmanship, to devise cunning works, to work in gold,
and in silver, and in brass, and in cutting of stones, to
set them, and in carving of timber, to work in all manner
of workmanship.' It was a marvelous revelation to me
that the Lord did have a gift of workmanship and art in
the Holy Spirit, and that what He had done for that man,

He could still do today. It has been a unique experience to sit at the desk day-by-day and sense the intimate promptings and 'checks' of the Holy Spirit in preparing and laying out a magazine—what to put in and what not to put in. I have no claim to laurels in art or journalism. The thing I am turning out isn't worthy of a gold seal of merit in an art show, but it is still a miracle because of what He has had to work with."

However others would by no means endorse those last remarks. North American *Floodtide* is a startlingly good piece of work, original, eye-catching, driving straight for its worldwide literature objective.

Peter Smith, who is now in charge of the Sales Department, came over from England with his wife and two children, where they had joined the C.L.C. This was after Peter's service in the army as a captain in World War II and ten years in the business world. In comparing C.L.C. in Britain with the work in the U.S.A. he says, "I found these much alike. They both were a lot different from any other business concern I had been with. The most noticeable thing is the absence of the profit motive, and the stress on souls rather than sales. On both sides of the ocean I have had to use a pick and shovel, and in England I had to carry a hundred-pound bag of potatoes on my back up five floors to the kitchen at Ludgate Hill.

"My training in the London packing room in the basement remains my strongest memory, because it was impressed upon us that we were in a warfare with the powers of darkness as we sent out books to radiate light. Each package not only had to be packed well, but was sent on its way with a prayer that the Holy Spirit would speak through the books. I enjoyed that packing-room fellowship and learned for the first time of the need for discipline in conversation. If we were too flippant or stopped work to talk, we were well-lectured by the brother in charge. He wanted us to be sober-minded workmen of God in the tradition of John Wesley.

"Books have certainly changed my life as they have for many others. Hardly a week goes by without someone reporting blessing in his life from reading one of our books. I am still thrilled with the opportunity of serving the church of Christ with books that change lives."

Irene Cagle keeping the books, Reg and Lily Fife in charge of Mail Order, Effie Smith handling the *Floodtide* circulation, Dave and Delores Shaver in mail order and secretarial work, Tom Fagan, ex-Ivory Coast missionary, on the road from his home on the west coast, form the U.S.A. team, augmented by new recruits preparing for the fields and faithful volunteer workers called 'over-timers.'

A generous gift from close friends of the C.L.C. in Canada made it possible to open a bookstore in Montreal as a base for Quebec and the Maritime Provinces, the Dominion's neediest and most populous area. Vyvyan Evans and his wife, Marjorie, pioneered this advance, with Marjorie also reaching many of the markets and fairs of Quebec by bookmobile. When ill health and other circumstances caused the Evanses to feel it was impossible to continue, John and Mary Ann Gross from the U.S. took over the Montreal work. The ministry from this center continues to go forward with many encouragements. The latest development has been a 50,000 French edition of the story of Father Chiniquy made possible by the generous cooperation of the Life Messengers, Incorporated of Seattle, Washington.

Years have passed, but the newer Crusaders still have to walk the tightrope of faith just as much as the older ones did in the early days; and it must always be so if C.L.C. is going to continue as a genuine work of faith— a business, but God's business, God-guided, God-run, God-supplied. One of the newest recruits accepted for the field by Fort Washington recently set out on a journey to the Middle West to prepare for going overseas. His letter back to Fort Washington gives a little glimpse into what could be repeated a hundred times over in the letters from Crusaders anywhere.

"The night before I was to leave Camp Hill, I had $9 left after having the car serviced and gassed up. In the morning $13 more came in just before I pulled out of the drive at 4 o'clock. This took care of gas and turnpike tolls to Chicago, with $1.69 left for the trip on to Nebraska and Minnesota. I stayed overnight there with a sister.

"The next morning I put $1.50 worth of cheap gas in my near-empty tank and started for Nebraska. I knew the Lord was still leading and would provide, but couldn't see how. About the time my fuel gauge was getting near empty again Peoria, Illinois and the name of a Bible school chum who had lived there, began to impress themselves on my mind. I couldn't shake off the thought so, thinking the Lord might be saying something, I stopped the car and consulted the map to see where in Illinois Peoria was. It was fifty miles south of my route and I had long since passed the highway I should have · taken to get there. So I concluded it was just a stray thought and continued toward Nebraska.

"I did tell the Lord to make it unmistakably plain if He did want me in Peoria for something. After driving quite a while the highway suddenly came to a dead end. I knew I must have missed the main road somewhere. Ahead was a narrow, icy crossroad with a small sign pointing one way, saying 'Putnam-Peoria.'

"The Spirit seemed to witness through it, so I turned down the icy road. It became worse and finally turned on to a wider but even more slippery road. I was travelling this when the car went into a skid and plunged down into the ditch. Here I sat, hopelessly stuck on a deserted road, the tank now registering flat empty, and 19¢ in my pocket. When I had finished counting my 'blessings' and got out of the car to look around I found a government snowplow already stopping to hook a chain onto my bumper. The Lord spoke again through a verse He had been giving me, 'The Lord looketh from heaven; he beholdeth all the sons of men.' Psalm 33:13, and I knew again that I was still in His will.

"Finally I came out on a highway which I could either take north to Nebraska or south to Peoria. Again the Spirit witnessed 'Peoria' so I turned south. A sign said thirty-seven miles to go and my gas gauge was so far back it had not even moved for about ten miles. I knew now though that He did want me in Peoria and so I began praising the Lord out loud for getting me there.

"I arrived in Peoria to discover about ten people listed in the phone book with the same name as my friend. I knew the only place I would have his address would be in my Bible school yearbook. I was sure I didn't have that, as I had only taken along books I expected to need, yet, there at the bottom of a suitcase, I found it. I discovered he actually lived in another smaller town five miles on the other side of Peoria. Well, I found the place and found my friend there serving a pastorate out in the country.

"Almost his first words after recovering from the shock of seeing me were, 'Can you stay over Sunday? We need a missionary speaker for this month.' I spoke in his church Sunday morning and in another church to both young people and adults in the evening. Also someone offered to do my prayer letters. A tentative booking for a three-day missionary conference was made, and $35 was given to me to continue my journey. The attendant at the filling station put fourteen and nine-tenth gallons in my fifteen gallon tank. The car had never so much as coughed!

"I finally arrived in Nebraska. Here again opportunities opened up for speaking and more gifts came in. I was able to get the winter coat I had asked the Lord for while in Pennsylvania. I had also asked for another white shirt, and the Lord woke up a woman in Nebraska City with the thought that she should buy me a white shirt. She didn't know but what I had a hundred shirts, but she knew the Lord's voice and obeyed.

"After figuring things out, I discovered that the Lord had sent in over $90 from the time I left Chicago until I arrived home in Blackduck, Minnesota. That makes just over $10 for every one I had the Wednesday night before I left Fort Washington. I don't know if that has some connection with a tithe in reverse or not, but I praise the Lord."

19

AUSTRALIA, THE THIRD HOME BASE

A spark from the Belgian Congo set the C.L.C. alight in Australia. All W.E.C. workers know Mary Rees, the fish girl from Liverpool, who raided the witchcraft dens of the Congo forests as boldly as she had bandied repartee with the crowds on a Saturday night in the city market. On one furlough she asked leave of no one, but packed her bag and started off on a tour to use that same smart tongue to tell the world what God was doing in the heart of Africa. "Miss Bullets" they called her in Congo, and she fired them with as true an aim at sleepy Christians at home. In Australia, she sold the W.E.C. magazine and booklets wherever she went. She met an industrial chemist who was on the W.E.C. council in Sydney, and scored a bull's eye. Conrad Lieber, with his wife Dorothy, caught the literature vision and started work in their home town, Blaxland. His first literature vehicle was a wheelbarrow used for carrying parcels of *C.T. Studd* from the post office!

With the birth of the C.L.C. the Liebers caught the world vision and commission. When released from his essential work in World War II (he worked for a major rubber manufacturing company at Granville) they took the big step from a salaried position to living by faith with a family of two small children, and founded the C.L.C. in Australia.

The start was a small room in the W.E.C. Headquarters at Ashfield, Sydney, with a kitchen cabinet as bookshelves.

From there they moved to a fourth floor room in a strategic location in the city, then to a bigger third floor room, then to a large basement with a direct access to the main street in the heart of the city, where basements of this kind are often shopping centers. More recently has come the purchase of a nine-acre property in Eastwood, a suburb of Sydney, where a complete C.L.C. Headquarters is to be built for staff, candidates, missionaries on furlough, mail order, printing and offices. The need is already obvious since Crusade workers on foreign fields from Australia now total fifteen, in addition to five from New Zealand. New Zealand also has its full-time C.L.C. representative in the person of Alec Thorne who founded the W.E.C. work in Spanish Guinea, West Africa. Now when over seventy years of age he has taken on this responsibility with much success.

Book distribution centers in Australia are supplied through the District Representative scheme. This is especially useful in a country of such vast distances, where the main cities are catered for, but where in the country districts and most of the large towns, it is not possible to buy Bibles, devotional books or Sunday School supplies. Businessmen, farmers, teachers, housewives and missionaries among the aborigines have all been used on a voluntary basis as distributors. At Tamworth and Goulbourn committees of Christians sponsor book centers. Fullscale C.L.C. centers have been opened in Parramatta, and in the far north in Townsville and Cairns.

Parramatta got its worker from London. Elizabeth Robertson felt a call to Australia, yet it seemed strange to transfer from one home base to another. So she asked the Lord for a threefold seal: a shop offered in a new town, for Con Lieber to write to London telling them of this and that he would mention the need for personnel. All of this happened and the call was confirmed. A Christian printer acquainted with C.L.C. and the need for premises, was looking for a press and saw an advertisement in Parramatta. He investigated only to find that the owner of the press had left and the premises were for rent. The real estate agent, a Christian, then offered the two rooms to the Crusade. That news, relayed to London, was the call.

Starting in these two back rooms (one had been a kitchen and the other a laundry) wasn't very inviting. Parramatta is a rapidly growing town, listed as making the biggest advance in the southern hemisphere, so Elizabeth was on the watch for better premises. For two years she waited, the little shop prospering and souls being saved; and then things began to move. Surrounding buildings were being demolished. Big Sydney businesses were buying property for huge sums. "Where," she asked, "in this rapidly expanding city, would C.L.C. find a shop in a central position? We did not have money to pay a large sum, but the Lord gave the assurance that He would work. Macquarie Street began to be transformed from a side street into a main street, and soon we heard that the Sunday School Hall next door had been condemned and a block of modern shops was to replace it. We applied for a shop, and amid the dust and rubble continued to believe that one would be ours. When the new building was nearing completion, we received a letter from the Methodist Trust saying that the shops were to be let and we could now apply. We continued to trust the Lord. A few weeks later another letter arrived to say they had reduced the premium to half and, to our great joy, we were granted a shop. We stepped out in faith for the high rent. Weekly God's blessing was on this step of faith, and it was not long before the shop was able to meet the rent."

Two thousand miles to the north is a mission field—Cairns, the most northerly city in Queensland, and gateway to the Tropical Wonderland of the north. Here the varied splendor of the jungle and sugar cane fields, the coral gardens of the Great Barrier Reef, the tumbling waterfalls and serene crater lakes of the Atherton Table-lands make it a popular tourist center. Albert and Martha Darbyshire had already been pioneer missionaries in the mountains of Azad, Kashmir and, after three years at Sydney Headquarters, they and their little family established themselves at Cairns. They took with them a very necessary bookmobile—the combined gift of a missionary, another friend, a sheep farmer and market gardener. Distribution covers a wide area, right up to the isolated parts of Cape York where in many cases the gospel has never been heard and where the people only meet at local race meetings from their "outback" cattle stations. But they have faithful co-workers who seize every opportunity to distribute tracts among the race-goers, picture-show crowds and drinkers. "The battles and difficulties have all been worthwhile," report the Darbyshires. They have now extended south, to Townsville, a city of 50,000 with Elizabeth Robertson transferring from Parramatta in charge. The greatest need is a Holy Ghost revival with an outpouring of His Spirit on this dry and thirsty north Queensland.

The first C.L.C. overseas field to be opened from Australia, in fellowship with New Zealand, has been New Guinea by two New Zealanders, Maurice and June Thomas. The coming of the Crusade to New Guinea met with much acceptance, and Maurice Thomas writes: "It is wonderful to see the way opening up before us. It certainly was the right time to open this field. Any later would have been too late as we are in on the ground floor of the expansion of this country. I believe that this is one of the first fields the Crusade has opened where we are ahead of the Communists and cults; but it may not be for long, because as soon as people become better educated, we will have the same problem as in other countries."

In Port Moresby, the capital of Papua where C.L.C. is located, the London Missionary Society, the oldest and largest mission there, has many churches and good congregations. They have opened all of these churches to the C.L.C. ministry.

In an air tour, Maurice found the same acceptance in every place. "In the Solomon Islands," he writes, "the missionaries said that it was the right time to make an advance with literature in this area. They took a number of the books and gave me a large order for more with the promise of being our distributing point in that part of the Solomons."

In the island of New Britain, at Rabaul, Maurice met a missionary of the Methodist Mission, and writes: "Rev. Lutton, a fine evangelical Christian, was enthusiastic about the idea of selling Christian literature. His mission has a shop on the main street of Rabaul and has been selling local publications only. I had taken with me two suitcases and two cardboard cartons full of books. When Rev. Lutton saw the books, he bought the lot on the spot and gave me an order for more. This should be a very good center as the Methodist mission is the biggest in this area."

Concerning Madang on the main island of New Guinea, Maurice writes: "The only mission in this area is the Lutherans. A visit to their station resulted in another warm welcome and a large order. The Lutheran mission is the largest in New Guinea with hundreds of workers and stations and they will have plenty of opportunity to distribute the literature among the natives."

In Lae, the next point of call, "again the Lutherans are the only missionaries in this area. The man in charge is a German and was a little cautious until I explained several ways of getting the books out, such as booktables and bookstalls outside their churches at times of meetings. They get crowds of between nine hundred and a thousand every week. These suggestions resulted in getting a goodly order from him.

"While I was away, a friend from Wewak wrote to us to see if he could act as our agent there. This was the only port at which I was unable to call on the trip.

"Recently we have sent off a supply of books to Daru in the Western District, where a doctor's wife has agreed to act as an agent for us. For all these openings and the cooperation of the various missions we give the Lord praise."

20

NATIONALS TAKE THE LEAD

In 1941 the W.E.C. sent missionaries to the little island of Dominica in the West Indies. The leader was an Australian, John Davey; his wife was a Canadian, the former Ethel Rodway. As news of the C.L.C. developments spread through W.E.C. ranks, John wrote Ken Adams of God's challenge to them to do something in literature in Dominica, and asked if C.L.C. would help. The missionaries were living in an upstairs room in Roseau, the capital of the island. The ground floor was occupied by a rum store and saloon, which meant plenty of wild goings on beneath the apartments. Prayer changed that and the store became empty just at the time God was speaking to them about literature. So in 1947 the plunge was taken and the downstairs made ready for a bookstore. The store has been there ever since. Later, plans changed for John and Ethel and they were succeeded by Olea Solheim, whom the mission would not accept because she was over sixty years of age. Olea, in real crusader spirit, went out on her own, and after spending some time helping in the bookstore, reapplied on the field and soon took over the full responsibility of the literature center in Dominica. Later she spent some time in Barbados and then went to help Lizzie Miller in St. Lucia. Sometimes over-age folk apply to a mission and are depressed and disgruntled when turned down, but what can be done with the rare ones who say, "Very well, I'll get there anyhow because God has told me to go," and so get in by the back door?!

Three years later John Davey met Ken in the U.S.A., and shared with him that his burden was not merely literature for Dominica, but for the whole of the West Indies. Correspondence and consultation crystallized into a decision. It was God's time to launch the C.L.C. in the islands and John would lead the way. But in which of the two leading islands should the start be made—Trinidad or Jamaica? John chose Trinidad and Ken joined him for a short while to help get the work established.

On the way to Trinidad Ken stopped for a night in Jamaica. There he contacted Harold Wildish, who had been his Sunday School teacher in England, and who was well known throughout the island as an evangelist and Bible teacher. It was one of those hairbreadth contacts which seem so little and mean so much, when God is in it. Before flying from Miami, a Christian business friend had told Ken he would see him at the airport and give him some introductions. Delayed by business, he contacted Ken by telephone just before he boarded the plane, and gave him the address of a Mr. Forbes in Jamaica. On arrival Ken phoned him and, in casual conversation, asked if he knew Wildish. He said not only did he know him but he was there in the island, and he put Ken in touch with him.

Harold Wildish, delighted and surprised at this unexpected call from Ken, drove to his hotel and then gave him a quick tour of Kingston during the two hours before the plane left. He showed him several of the recently built Gospel Halls of the Brethren and then finished with the direct personal challenge: "Ken, you must come back for a visit and you must bring your literature program to Jamaica. For some years now, both missionaries and national Christians here have been greatly burdened. Jamaica is the headquarters of the Seventh-Day Adventists for the whole of West Indies. Jehovah's Witnesses are active, moving from one end of the island to the other. As a result we are seeing some of our converts led astray by their literature. Apart from a very small supply of literature which a few of us missionaries have brought in, there is no evangelical literature in this island of Jamaica. I urge you to come and do something about it."

"It's a tremendous challenge, Harold," Ken acknowledged, "but frankly I'm just on my way to Trinidad and that's our next job. I don't know that we can do anything for a year or two."

"Oh," he said, "can't you return on your way back from Trinidad? I'll arrange meetings every night of the week and also make other contacts for you."

He was really in earnest about it and Ken promised to return if at all possible. "It did prove possible," recalls Ken, "and I was able to spend eight days in Jamaica on my way back from Trinidad.

"My plane arrived about 6 o'clock. Mr. Sanguinetti, a business man, was at the airport to meet me. 'I'm glad your plane is on time,' he said, 'we have a meeting for you at 7 o'clock.' It was the regular weekly prayer meeting of one of the Kingston Assemblies and about 300 people had gathered.

" 'This is a fine turn-out,' I said to one of them.

" 'This is our regular crowd,' he answered. 'We didn't know whether you were coming or not. No one is here especially to hear you!'

" 'This is wonderful,' I replied. 'You mean to say 300 people come to the weekly prayer meeting?'

" 'Yes, God is blessing us down here in Jamaica.'

"Here was evidence indeed of what Harold Wildish had told me. I spoke for about an hour, and shared with them the opportunities I had seen down in Trinidad and in some of the other islands."

George daCosta, a Jamaican of forty years of age, was in that meeting. He had been born and brought up a Roman Catholic. Not until he was twenty-five years old did he have his first contact with the gospel. "It was just before we got married," he said. "In Jamaica you have beautiful nights with the moon glistening and the trees seeming to glisten in return, and if you're by the sea it's a marvelous sight. I was there walking with the young lady who is now my wife and we heard some singing. To her it sounded good and she suggested we stop and listen. When we turned the corner we saw a big tent and a man preaching and another giving out several 'Hallelujahs.' This sounded strange to me and I said, 'Ah, come on, Blanche. I don't want to hear anything like that. It's utter rubbish.' Of course, she was intent on getting her man, so she just obeyed me! Little did I know that in a short time I would be preaching the same gospel and saying many a 'Hallelujah.'

"I was then working with Issa's, a multi-million-pound firm in Jamaica. A young woman came to work in my department and Blanche and I become very friendly with the family. She was a dear Christian girl and invited us to hear the gospel. By then we had had our first child and Blanche couldn't go, so I said I would go just to please her, although it was strictly against my religion. I went, and that night for the first time in my life heard the gospel. I was then thirty-one years old. Also for the first time in my life I held a Bible in my hand and opened it. I knew nothing about the Word of God. I'd never seen my parents pray. The man was preaching about the cross, and about Christ bearing our sins in His own body. For the second time I became really 'R.C.' (Really Convicted), and at the end of that service I knew that I was 'R.C.' (Really Converted). I saw Christ dying for me. I knew that I was a guilty one. I knew that I should have borne the punishment and the tears just rolled down my cheeks as I sat in that place. I went home and as Blanche opened the door I said, 'You know, Blanche, something has happened. Christ died for me.'

" 'Didn't you know that all the while?' she asked.

" 'Yes, but it's different tonight, He died for *me*, personally.'

"Next morning I bought myself a Bible. It was just an ordinary Bible and had no references or anything. Within a week I bought a Scofield Bible. We lived with my parents at the time. One day Dad and I were going out to work and I said to him, 'By the way, I bought myself another Bible.'

" 'What! You bought *another* Bible,' he exclaimed. 'How much?'

" 'Eight dollars,' I replied.

" 'Are you crazy?' he asked. 'You have a young family and you'd waste $8 on another Bible?'

"I looked at him and said, 'How much did you lose in playing poker last night?' He couldn't answer."

Much as in Ken Adams' early life, God was preparing a literature agent in George daCosta. He continued to work at Issa's and was promoted to an important position in the firm. But having been starved of the Word of God himself, as he witnessed to people he felt a constant urge to get the Scriptures into their hands. He used his influence with the firm to get a book department started and was able to introduce Bibles and evangelical books into this Catholic firm. Then he began to set up booktables at gospel campaigns, paying for literature out of his own pocket and giving the profits to the Brethren Assemblies. He also persuaded some Assemblies to institute bookcases and booktables.

Then came the prayer meeting at which Ken spoke. Harold Wildish, who knew of George's concern for literature, had particularly invited him to that meeting. George talked with Ken afterward and told him of his burden for literature, and that what Ken had said was a tremendous challenge to him.

"But, I have a wife and four children," he said. Wisely, Ken did not press or even encourage him.

"You will have to go carefully," he told him, "and

watch for God in this. C.L.C. would certainly be interested in seeing some development but, you know, we are not offering you a job."

Ken found out later that this remark quite offended him—and quite justfiably we think! C.L.C. has learned through the years that it is usually better to discourage an applicant, for those who persist are likely to be those who are really called.

Some months later, George took the final step. An elderly Jamaican lady had a small store, a kind of ice cream counter, where she also kept a few books—the only evangelical Christian bookstore in Jamaica. By means of a loan of £1,000 from a Christian brother—which showed what confidence there was in George—he was able to buy and obtain additional stocks of literature.

"After working many years with the Issa firm," continues George, "and ten years after I was saved, I talked with the boss and told him how the Lord was leading.

" 'You're not serious about this are you, after twenty years?' he asked. 'What is it? How much do you want?'

" 'Nothing,' I said, 'I'm going to serve the Lord.'

"He looked at me, placed his hand on my knee and said, 'George, I know if you say "nothing," you mean "nothing." ' "

But it was still step by step. George and Blanche introduced a special hobby of his into the store—making little nick-nacks, souvenirs for which there is a great demand in the island. George was clever with his hands at this kind of thing. He wrote and asked Ken to be a sort of director and to give advice, although the work would not actually be linked with C.L.C. This Ken did by willingly supplying stock, but also warning him: "George, the Lord bless you and prosper you, but as you have asked me to be a director and give you counsel, I want to pass this word on to you. I don't believe you will be able to do the two things. You won't be able to properly run this nicknack department and the literature

department too. One will take priority. The other will
take a back seat. I believe if God is calling you and has
led you out of business into a life of faith, it surely must
be to promote His gospel through the printed page, and
not to fiddle around with nicknacks."

They certainly were tested from the start. The great
Jamaica hurricane in 1951 hit them the night the first
consignment of books arrived. "Next morning the ceilings
had fallen down, the water had poured in, and we had
a loss of a couple of hundred pounds to start with," says
George. "We had four children to take care of and now
this new business seemed wrecked from the very begnning.

"My mother looked at me that evening when we told
her what we were doing and said, 'You're a fool, George.
You're a disgrace to the family. After working right to the
top, you're going to cast your children upon charity.'

" 'No, Mama,' I said, 'not charity—upon God.'

"Needless to say the priest and various ones all gave
us a difficult time. But we went on. We had a little money
when we surrendered our three insurance policies, which
we felt the Lord didn't want us to keep now that we were
trusting Him. But up until then we hadn't stepped out
to trust the Lord fully. We were still believing that we
could go and earn money and give to God. But God was
still wanting us to give *ourselves* to Him—not just our
money. Then we began to see that our time was being
taken up more with the secular work because we had
to meet rentals, and the literature ministry was falling
into the background. Yet God was blessing the secular
work and we were making money. This we couldn't understand. We had to get to the Lord about it.

"Soon God showed us clearly that what He wanted
was lives fully given over to Him, surrendered to get His
Word out. There was nothing like this in Jamaica before
—very little Christian literature work at all. So we prayed
about this matter again and the Lord impressed us with
the thought of inviting John Davey to Jamaica. He came

and we took him all over the island, introducing him to many people. John did a tremendous job speaking in the churches.

"When he was ready to go, I said, 'Now, John, here's the point. We're in two businesses. We can't do both. We want you to take over the literature part of the work. We'll even give you the shop and get back into our old job or carry on our private business.' I shall never forget that night.

"John looked at me and said, 'George, C.L.C. will never do that. We believe God has called *you* to this job and we are going to wait on God to show this to you clearly.'

"Soon after, the Lord made clear to us what we should do, so we went on our knees and told Him, 'If Issa could take care of us and supply our needs, then Lord You can do it. So we hand over everything to You now.' We wrote Ken and John and got rid of all the secular things in the shop. Then we handed over the rest to C.L.C., and the Lord began to pour out His blessing in a way that has been unbelievable.

"He also led us into bookmobile work. We had never known a thing about this, but started moving around the island taking books to the market places. The response was amazing. Any time of the day we could drive up to a market or park on an estate, start playing the gospel records on the public address system, and hundreds would come around to receive the tracts and Gospels we were handing out. Enclosed in each Gospel would be an invitation for a free Bible correspondence course. Today, we have over 27,000 studying these courses in the islands. The Source of Light Mission now takes care of this correspondence ministry. We found the bookmobile ministry one of the greatest phases of this work, because we could meet people who wouldn't go to a church. They would be too tired after working in the fields, and too lazy to wash and dress, but they would stand around and hear the gospel.

"One afternoon, for instance, a man gave his testimony in a church where I was preaching. 'Two years ago I was walking along a country road and a van came along with some books in it. A man jumped out and asked if I could tell him the way to a certain town. After I had told him, the man gave me a Gospel of John and said, "You go home and read this Gospel and I'll be praying that the Holy Spirit will lead you to know Christ as your Saviour." I went home and read it and was gloriously saved right in my room.' Then he pointed to me and said, 'And there is the man who gave me that Gospel.' You can imagine the thrill of such a thing.

"One evening another man stopped me and said, 'Sir, you are giving out the Word of God.'

" 'Yes,' I said.

" 'Praise God for that,' he said, 'I work in a cattle shed. One day while sitting in that shed I saw a piece of paper on the ground. I picked it up and read these words: "As for me and my house, we will serve the Lord." I threw it down and then picked it up again, and suddenly God said, "You are not serving Me, much less your family, your house." I just burst out in tears and claimed Christ as my Saviour.'

"Such encouragements were not ours alone. The churches started to realize the need, and a few of us got together and drafted a circular to all the ministers in the island. Soon we started getting invitations for meetings. Then schools became interested, and today we have openings into the high schools and in the University and among the nurses. The Lord continually saved souls and encouraged our hearts in the work.

"God began adding workers, local and foreign, to the fellowship. This enabled us to open a second store—in Montego Bay—and it is filling a tremendous need. We also go out to the estates from there with a bookmobile. In Mandeville, in the very center of the island, where the West Indies Mission Bible School is located, we have our third book shop with a Jamaican worker in charge.

"In the meantime, John Davey had been forwarding the work in the other islands. The start had already been made in Dominica; the work there is now manned by Helga Hotvedt, Meredith Nelson and Cornelia John Baptiste. From there the work has expanded into Trinidad, where Bill and Evelyn Johnston and Eileen Turton are in charge of two bookstores and a mobile ministry. Hudson and Geraldine Chang (from Jamaica) are in British Guiana. The John Daveys direct the work in Barbados. In British Honduras with its 95 per cent Roman Catholicism, God has established a C.L.C. testimony. (This work is slowly being rebuilt as all was lost in the 1961 Hurricane Hattie). St. Lucia, one of the most spiritually difficult islands, was recently entered and this work is under the supervision of Lizzie Miller and Olea Solheim. Antigua also has been entered with Phyllis Trim working there. We are now established in St. Kitts, with Sylvia Wallace from Jamaica currently in charge. Grenada and Tobago are the next targets for C.L.C., and we have had calls from Bermuda, Nassau and other places. We believe that this is God's time for this ministry, and even if we wear our bodies out, we intend to move on. The time is ripe to work in these small islands, so difficult previously because of illiteracy. The educational program is being pushed, and in almost every town you can find new schools opened and new literates made. We believe God wants us to buy up every opportunity."

Has the Lord supplied for those four children the daCostas had when they left the business and Ken warned them to be sure before they stepped out on faith? "We have found right along the way that God has supplied," says George. "To give you just one personal example, we had three girls in high school. High school is very expensive in Jamaica and you have to pay the tuition fees during the first week of every term, or the child isn't allowed to continue. On one occasion we didn't have the money to send with them to school, nevertheless we sent them in faith. 'The Lord will do it,' we said. 'Everything is going to be all right and He will provide.' We felt everything was going to be all right. I am afraid we just took it for granted.

"Two weeks went by and then Betty, who is a very sensitive child, came in one evening and said, 'Daddy, every day Mrs. Clark asks if you gave me an envelope. Is it the fees?'

" 'Yes,' I said, 'it is.'

" 'Daddy,' she said, 'I feel ashamed to go and be asked every morning.'

"That night we went on our knees and I said to Blanche, 'I found out why God hasn't sent the school fees. We haven't asked him. We have taken Him for granted. God expects us as children to come to Him and make our needs known to Him.' So we told Him. In the morning when we went down to the bookstore and pushed up the shutters, we found an envelope on the floor. When we opened it there was some money and a little note which read: 'For the children's schooling.' Midday another brother sent us a little note, saying, 'God has just laid it on our hearts to send you this little gift toward the children's schooling.' By 4 o'clock in the afternoon a letter came from John Davey: 'We have just finished scraping the bottom of the barrel and found this $3 in a corner, and thought you might need it.' That completed the fees for the children's schooling. I can tell you as a testimony, we might fail God but He won't fail us.

"On one of our visits to British Honduras," continues George, "we had flown halfway to our destination and were just circling the Cayman Islands when a terrific storm started. In the lightning, thunder and rains the plane was being tossed about like a bit of paper in the air. Everybody became frantic. The man sitting in front of me kept ordering whisky and soda. A young woman

with her baby got hysterical. Many were crying. I sat
there at the back of the plane reading my Bible. A young
man sitting in the front got up and said, 'Friends, don't
be frightened. Nothing is going to happen to this plane.'
Everybody looked at him. I didn't even know he was on
the plane. He was one of the salesmen for the firm for
which I had worked many years before. He said, 'Nothing
is going to happen because there is a certain man on this
plane who is a Christian. I've worked with him for years
and he didn't just tell us he was a Christian, but he lived
before us as a Christian.' He suddenly lifted his hand
and pointed to me and said, 'That is the man and he is
reading his Bible and praying. Everybody was quiet for
a moment. This was an opportunity. And while the plane
tossed I took some Gospels and gave one to each, saying,
'Now, be quiet. Everything will be all right.' The pilot
tried for some three hours to bring the plane down in
the Cayman Islands, and each time the strong wind
howling across the runway made it impossible. So eventually he had to return to Jamaica.

The next day we took off again. Suddenly I heard the
bell ring from the pilot's cabin, and saw the stewardess
go forward. Soon she came out and said, 'I am sorry to
tell you that we are returning to Jamaica immediately.
It is nothing too serious, a valve is leaking. As long as
the valve holds out, it will be all right.' I need not tell
you the tension in the hearts of everyone. I was sitting
beside my salesman friend. Dinner time came and it was
my favorite meal, roast chicken. I ate every piece of it.
But I noticed he hadn't touched his.

" 'How in the world can you do that?' he asked.

" 'Man, it's good.' I replied.

" 'You want mine?'

" 'You're telling me!'

"So I had his as well. We got back to Jamaica around
3:30. I went into our book center and was having a
lemonade when one of our girls, Sheila, came in. She

threw her hands up, did a rightabout-turn and ran down the street, she was so frightened at seeing me. You know in Jamaica we say the 'duppy' is after you. She was as white as a sheet! Needless to say, all my friends said this was a sure and distinct warning that I should not go to British Honduras at this time. But to me this was a sure indication that God wanted me to go and get His work done. So the next day I went. At the terminal building, just before the flight was announced, all of us passengers were standing together. So I looked at them and said, 'Friends, listen. We have boarded this plane twice and haven't stood together and asked God to take us over. I wonder if you would mind if I prayed?' We bowed our heads and committed ourselves to the Lord, boarded the plane and flew beautifully across to British Honduras."

George daCosta has been one of several nationals, such as Kawai-san in Japan and Donald David in India, who, under the good guidance of C.L.C., have taken leadership in their countries. This is one of the healthiest signs of right development in the C.L.C. worldwide. It naturally produces more national representatives through the whole field. The first two Jamaican co-workers were Marjorie Smith and Sylvia Wallace. They were followed by George Webster (Jamaican), Jen Wong (Jamaican Chinese), Madge Bennett (Jamaican), Enid Hoo (Jamaican Chinese), Marion Manning (Barbadian), Irvine and Alva Robinson (British Honduran), and Geraldine and Hudson Chang (Jamaican Chinese).

Does this eliminate the need for more foreign missionaries? George answers that: "We still need missionaries—though your conception of missionaries might be different from mine. A missionary, as far as we in Jamaica are concerned, is someone who comes in and helps to do the work of God. A missionary to you may be one who goes out to an uncivilized country to bring the gospel to an uncivilized people. But today the world is larger than that, and you will find islands and countries which, though not in that category, are not yet missionary-minded and financially strong enough to support their own people on the field. The vision has not yet broken through into the hearts of the Christians, that you just give up your secular job and go out into the work. We have been getting the gospel for only a hundred years or so. In Britain and U.S.A. and other countries you have hundreds of years behind you when Christ has been made known and the implications of the gospel have been driven home. Yes we want missionaries. But they must come with a very open mind today. Whatever field they go to they are going to people who now have learned to think for themselves. They are not just natives, as the Americans and English previously thought of natives. Natives fifty years ago were considered uncivilized, illiterate underdogs. But that is not the meaning of the word native today. And the moment you come with that in your mind, or allow them to have the slightest thought that you have that in your mind, your witness is finished."

21

THE CARIBBEAN CHALLENGE

It is good to watch the innovations of the Spirit in every generation, new wine in new wineskins, adapting the age-old message to its modern environment, not in content but in presentation. Many such twentieth-century adaptations, evidence of the surging life of the Head through the members, could be named with thankfulness, despite the downcast looks of the pessimists who are constantly reading the burial service of the Church of Christ.

For one of these adaptations God had a young sports editor of a New Zealand newspaper, Trevor Shaw. With Christ in his heart he went to Nigeria with the idea of starting a magazine with a sufficiently contemporary and indigenous flavor to attract the non-religious, yet constantly containing the message of salvation in plain terms, and food and challenge for the Christians. This resulted, not only in launching the *African Challenge* magazine, which soon soared into a best seller and remained so, but the news of its success also resounded throughout the missionary world and many were quick to recognize in it a new approach to a new generation; and "Challenge-type" magazines began to appear in many mission fields.

Trevor Shaw had close personal links with C.L.C. Contacts with him, together with the interchange of ideas with the editorial staff of the *African Challenge* and others, brought the C.L.C. to the point of recognizing a call from God to do the same for the West Indies, to produce a *Caribbean Challenge*.

The start was in greatest human weakness, and we might almost add, as usual, with a woman! The one member of the C.L.C. staff in Britain with some slight editorial and reporting experience, was a young woman in her twenties—Thelma Cooper. The team who arrived in Jamaica in 1956 to start the magazine was Thelma as editor, Charlton Smith (later joined by his wife, Amy) to give a couple of years to the build-up of the art work, cover designs, format, etc., and Ken Adams to forge a chain of distributing agents throughout the islands.

"It was a memorable day in 1956 at Palisadoes Airport, Kingston, when Ken, Charlton and I stepped from the plane into Jamaica's simmering August heat," says Thelma. "The friendly brown-skinned immigration officer raised his eyebrows when he noticed 'missionary' written on my papers. 'Missionary? You think we are bad then?' he queried sharply. While I stuttered and tried to think how to answer, he cut me short with a swift: 'Well, we are! Welcome!'

"It was certainly no ordinary mission field to which I had come, and I swiftly learned to cut out of my conversation such words as 'national' and 'missionary." I soon found that there existed in the West Indies a solid core of men like George daCosta—men with the blood of Africa and Europe mingled in their veins, able to lead others and run things without outside interference. That was quite all right with me. I was quite incapable of running anything.

"It was fascinating to study Jamaicans in their own environment: so many skin shadings, so many feature gradings, so many beauties. Jamaican humor was something I had to get used to. It is quite Elizabethan—full-blooded and a bit slapstick. Woe betide you if you have no sense of humor in Jamaica!

"Jamaican hospitality is quite remarkable. As visitors, people made us so welcome that life could have been one long round of being entertained, but for the fact that we had work to do. And what work it proved! Hour₃ and hours of prayer, discussion, trudging round town, as Ken, George, John Davey, Charlton and myself hammered out future policies and methods for the magazine. We decided it should be called the *Caribbean Challenge*.

"We toured print shops seeking estimates. One printer gave us his price as over £800* per issue, and asked, 'How much capital do you have?'

" 'Five pounds given to us by a Christian,' we boldly replied. 'But God has much more in His "bank" for us.'

"He smiled cynically and said that he had had several before us who wanted to start magazines just to get their names and photos in print. Then after a few months they had had to fold up, leaving him to hold the bag.

" 'Then you're not the man God wants to do this job,' said Ken firmly.

"So next we went to the Offset Printing Company. There we found the cooperation we needed. It was then a small firm, but they agreed to take us on at a price nearer our figure. Over the years we have found them very helpful and tolerant of us, even when we've missed the deadline. Incidentally, God has blessed Offset too—Mr. Condell now prints several Jamaican magazines.

"We took possession of an editorial office which Mr. Gladstone Sanguinetti, a Christian builder, had generously offered rent-free. It was amusing to see our magazines when they first came off the press, stacked up in boxes in his long warehouse."

Their first problem was finance. "We realized one thing," Ken Adams says, "it was going to cost a lot of money. John Davey once commented, and I don't think he was altogether joking, 'Ken, I hope you have brought plenty of money with you to put this through!' I assured him I had brought plenty of faith, but in my wallet I had about $80 for my three months' visit to the West

(*To calculate British pounds in dollars, multiply by four to give an approximate value £1=$4)

Indies. The more we investigated and consulted together, the more we realized that we were launching on perhaps the largest single undertaking in C.L.C.'s history, calling for a minimum of £1,000 * per month.

"It was a real encouragement to us that the first gift of £5 came from a Jamaican Christian. This was used to send out a letter to key people in the islands informing them of the project and of my proposed visit. Apart from that, there was not much evidence of any adequate financial deliverance—and then things really began to happen.

"George daCosta came into the *Challenge* office one morning with a big broad grin on his face and a 'Praise the Lord' on his lips. A Christian brother had just handed him a check for £90 which he and his wife had been led to give. They had sold some property and this was a portion of the Lord's tithe. We rejoiced in that.

"Then a few days later I received a letter from our workers in Australia. From a recent gift they had received the Lord had led them to allocate £200 toward the *Caribbean Challenge*. We were much encouraged. A further letter came, this time from our colleagues in Britain, and I think our 'Hallelujah' was even louder because it told of a gift of £1,000 earmarked for the *Caribbean Challenge*. Friends in the United States also caught the vision and helped with their gifts, and the Evangelical Literature Overseas made a promise of $5,000.

"In one way and another we witnessed the Lord delivering us as we went forward in complete faith and dependence upon Him. Over the years the testimony has been the same. We had hoped the magazine would soon become self-supporting and I believe this could be done if we had more paid advertising, but up to the present it still needs an annual subsidy. Yet the testimony remains the same that God is providing."

"We had no equipment in those first months," recalls Thelma, "no filing cabinet, no fan or sun-blind to fight the grilling heat, no desks—no shelves to put anything on —just a couple of tables and a printing bill for nearly £750 to meet each month. The story of how God has supplied our needs, and still does, would fill a book by itself.

"The second big problem was personnel, or lack of it. Charlton was a source of strength on the art side. But I was 'X' the unknown quantity on the editorial side. No one felt this more than I. The job ahead looked frightfully big and I felt exceedingly small. We had no secretarial help, no other journalistic help and no full-time help with the business side of the magazine.

"Of course we had the assistance of the Jamaican C.L.C. team. George's help and encouragement pushed us through many a rough spot. Often he carried boxes of magazines from the printers, stacked them in his car and drove them down to the wharf for shipping.

"Local Christians helped too. We had the warehouse full of them on many occasions, helping to wrap the magazines for mailing. This was before we got properly organized on the distribution. Those days were hectic! Everybody did everything! Charlton and a team of local boys stuck posters on telephone poles, announcing the advent of *Challenge*. I tried to keep track of the banking. George went around with a big book in which distribution records were noted down, and tried to see that everybody got their roll of magazines on time. Eventually the Lord sent us Marion Manning from Barbados to handle distribution and keep accounts. She has been a tremendous asset to the team.

"The shortage of staff has been a continual headache these five years. First it was just Charlton and I. Then Amy Smith came. Then Marion. In June 1958 Julaine Smith came from the States for the art and layout, releasing Charlton and Amy who had been on loan from Britain. Since then the three of us have battled on. Three girls—'the weak things of this world, but mighty through

God.' Marion does a good job on the business side of the magazine. She has built up a happy family relationship with our distributors. Being a 'small islander' herself gives her an edge with them. Julaine does well on the art and layout despite increasing ill health. I struggle to hold up my part in the editorial chair, encouraged by George. Many times I have almost given up because I have felt I was more of a hindrance than anything. But gradually I have learned to be a conqueror in the fight. For nine months we were not three but two. Because of her health Julaine was on furlough (she has since returned). Yet the magazines came out just the same, with the verdict 'good as ever.' To Him be all the glory.

"Problem number three was ignorance. Now that I know something more about the islands, I really wonder at our temerity in starting operations on such a small fund of know-how. The islands are small and scattered, some separated by many miles of water. The magazine has to travel far to people with diverse aims and racial backgrounds, who are living under a common sun and learning to work together. We have to cater for the Indian, who looks back to 'Mother India'; to the African looking back to Africa; to the diverse 'colored' population who live very much within their own social framework and are learning a new West Indian nationalism. To help us get acclimated we started the Editorial Advisory Committee, composed of local Christian leaders. They give us much help and advice.

"The fourth major problem was lack of writers. In the beginning we knew of only one trained Jamaican Christian writer. How could we produce a magazine without writers? Ken went off on a promotional tour around the West Indies. His trip not only resulted in finding key men in each island for distribution, but also encouraged some to write.

"With the articles Ken sent back we began to put together the first issue due to appear in January 1957. It

sold well, mainly because of a lovely free calendar designed by Charlton. The February issue sold well because
of a free map of the area. Then came a slump, and a
battle to find a level of content that would meet the need.

"For almost two years we faced unabated criticism.
Then, somehow, we discovered the formula and the
magazine began to climb in popularity. Today, thank
God, we are still learning and still climbing.

"Out of the struggle and agony I have learned a few
things about getting articles from people. Most people
have a story locked inside them, in their lives, but they
may not have the ability to bring it out. The trained
journalist can interview them and collect the facts for a
story. One good source of article material is listening to
people's views on controversial issues. Some articles have
come out of discussions which took place on Jamaican
verandahs. Another thing I have learned is that people
can learn to write, for writing is both an art and a craft.
Out of my own struggles to perfect my technique I am
now able to help others.

"Bob Walker, Editor of *Christian Life* Magazine, conducted a writers' workshop in 1958 which helped many
of our young people get started on the typewriter. Now
we have quite a number who write for us. But there is
no relaxation. One always has to be on the stretch for
more. The alert editor has to listen constantly for casual
remarks such as: 'I was down in Trinidad the other day
and I met . . . He has a good story about something that
happened to him in . . .'"

"One man sent in a very 'preachy' article, with a note
at the bottom of his letter asking us to rejoice that his
false teeth which had been lost in the sea had been re-
stored to him on the third day in answer to prayer!
Needless to say I wrote back at once and got the story!

"What about results? Thousands of souls have been
touched through the magazine. Approximately one thousand write in every year for a Bible correspondence

course offered free in the magazine. Some letters tell us of souls saved through reading *Challenge*. Broken lives have been mended. In these islands men and women often live together out of wedlock. Articles on problems of immorality have struck home and brought some together in marriage.

"Thirty thousand copies a month—each one a missionary—each one of tremendous life-changing potential. How we need prayer that the edge will not be blunt—that the sickle may really reap the harvest which is ripe and waiting."

22

FORWARD TO AN ISLAND WORLD

Grace Chang was from China. For twenty-four years she served among the people of that great land, living as one of them. Intermittent home responsibilities in the States, and then the closing of the door when Communism over-ran the country, kept her from further missionary service but never dampened her spirit or lessened her desire to be back on the mission field. It was not until she was past sixty years of age that the new opportunity came and she joined the C.L.C.

She learned two significant lessons from her years in China which prepared her for this new commission as a literature pioneer. The first was complete trust in God. She had started on her way to China as an independent missionary with five dollars in her pocket and no train or boat ticket. She ended her years of service in China, landing back in New York with $45 in hand. All along the way the Lord had abundantly provided. So, as she said, she returned nine times better off!

Secondly she had been deeply moved by seeing the satisfaction of illiterate people as they learned to read and the joy when, for the first time, they could stand up in church and read their own Bibles. Now, when preaching in China is often forbidden, the fact that many Chinese Christians have and can read their Bibles is what is helping to hold them true today.

What had God for her future? Where was her next field of service to be? Could God still provide as He had done so faithfully in days gone by? What bothered her was that wherever she went people would say, "Where are you going to raise your support? How are you going to get money for this or that?" Has the Lord changed, she would ask herself? Do people talk of faith in a different way now?

A contact with Ken Adams brought her to the Fort Washington Headquarters. She did not know much about the Crusade but came for a week-end conference. "I was given a meal," she said, "and they did not set a price for it. At the meetings they didn't take a collection. I did not know who these people were, but I was amazed that they prepared meals for so many visitors and did not ask for anything." That drew her to W.E.C. She saw "this funny crowd of people in their shirt sleeves in the meeting. It didn't look much like a church service, but when I heard the messages, that was enough. I went back to Philadelphia, got my suitcase and returned to hear more."

And there she stayed—neither guest nor candidate. At one meeting she heard Ken Adams give a message on "willing hands," and that's what she offered to be. "I was just 'willing hands,'" she comments. "I helped in C.L.C. doing about every job there was to be done. I knew the Lord was preparing me for something, but I never thought it was going to be for the foreign field again. I must have been at headquarters, on and off, for almost a year and a half. During that time there was a public conference with Roy Hession, author of *The Calvary Road,* and other speakers. Mrs. Adams came to me and said, 'Grace, will you take over the kitchen and do the buying and cooking for 300 people?' It is not a surprise to be asked as a candidate to do such things, but I wasn't a candidate! I wasn't anything—just a 'blower-in' and a 'blower-out,' as Ken used to call me, because every once in a while I would go off for a few days and then return. As I could not refuse, I agreed to do the best I could. Mrs. Adams said, 'There is just one thing, Grace, we must have the meals on time.' About the only thing I was afraid of after coming from China was the American clock. I just could not take the push of having to get something done by the clock. I could not take it in my own home, to say nothing of cooking for 300 people. But the Lord wonderfully undertook. So much so that instead of helping in the kitchen for this one five-day conference, I found myself in the kitchen for five different conferences in one year!"

She had one door open to her which would give her a position of security, but suddenly the Lord told her to "lie down and not move a finger." She did not dare disobey. "I call it the 'stop light of God' and one of the most precious things in my life. It is one thing for the Lord to give us a green light, but when the Lord says 'stop' and He doesn't show you one further step ahead, that is another story. I praise the Lord for the Crusade. They didn't know me nor understand me, but they surely recognized that the Lord was leading in my life."

Then came a clear and sudden call to Indonesia. "How marvelously God had worked. He had put me in a hot kitchen, He had given me a time clock I was afraid of and He had allowed me to work long hours through the heat of July. When I came up for acceptance by the C.L.C., the Staff couldn't say I was too old or that I would not be able to take the heat, for they had already given me the hottest job on the hill!" How neatly God fits into a working community those of His choice who don't conform to normal standards of acceptance, when free fellowship is more its basis than officialdom.

The old warrior was accompanied to Java by one co-worker, a young man, Willard Stone—an unusual pair to start and build C.L.C. in those islands of such vast opportunity. At first they stayed in the W.E.C. Headquarters at Kediri in East Java. "I had a little room in what the Indonesians call a pavilion, but what would be more like a garage to us. The front was a bookroom.

I slept and studied in the back. I praise the Lord for that little bookroom, for it was there that I got one of my first impressions of Indonesia as I looked at the expressions on the faces of the people when they picked up the books. The Chinese would pick them up with a smile, and those who understood English were happy. But for the Indonesians there was very little in their language. When Sunday school teachers came in there was no picture material for them to buy for the children. They looked so sad. The Indonesians are a quiet people and would not say anything, but they would turn away with such a sad look. It revealed the unspoken question, 'Why was so little available for them.' The Lord impressed that look on my heart, and I said, 'Lord, by Your help I will do something for the children of Indonesia!' "

By 1956 they were ready to start a full-scale literature ministry. But the first problem was accommodation. Surabaja, the second largest city in Indonesia, with a million in population, was their objective. "Indonesia is a land of ninety-six million people, and in large cities everything is so crowded that it is next to impossible to obtain premises for a bookstore. Such problems can only be conquered by prayer. For three long months Willard searched in Surabaja but always came back weary and unsuccessful. Then we found two rooms. We felt these would do for a start and planned that the little front room would contain the bookroom and one of us would live in the back room. We have often laughed since as we see the present store and the books stacked to the ceiling."

How casually things "seem" to happen. The day before signing for these rooms Grace Chang was invited to a Chinese home. During the visit a Chinese gentlemen came in unexpectedly. Hearing why they were coming to Surabaja, and about the two rooms, he said, "No one will find you there. If you want to sell Bibles and Christian books you may use the front of my store." That man had only come into the room to telephone. "Who but God sent him into the room just at that moment?" says Grace. When she returned that night to the Chinese pastor and his wife where she was staying, they said, "If he has said that, take it, for we have been praying about that place for six months, but did not dare to ask him for it." It turned out that they were his relatives but, being just poor preachers and he a rich businessman, they did not wish to ask a favor of him. "So next morning at 7 o'clock I was at his house," says Grace. "I asked him what he wanted for the rent, and he said we could have it free. So for five years we had this store rent free, with light and telephone supplied. It was equipped with glass cases and chairs. We had nothing to do but put the books on the shelves. To make the outreach of Christian literature possible, the Lord had worked a miracle and given us a store in what might be called the 'hub of opportunity.' It was situated in the second largest city of Indonesia, on one of the busiest streets, ten minutes from the main post office, three minutes from the bus station and a short distance from the seaport. Who but God could put us in such a place?"

The outreach from one little bookstore with two workers has been like the five loaves and two fishes. "In the first year in Surabaja," says Grace, "the sales were $18,500. We had about 300 accounts, but only thirty-five of them were in the city. All the others were from fifty cities in Java and ten other islands. Because of the strategic location, people came to the store from other islands. Some would fly over, some came by train, others by boat. It is marvelous what the Lord has done, giving us such a great outreach from this one bookstore. Thousands of books are going out, but when one thinks of ninety-six million people it is just a trickle. We cannot keep enough supplies on hand, so we do not send out a catalog, but just a printed sheet listing the latest books. We feel the next advance will be a bookmobile to reach the country

churches and the people in the villages. The island of
Java alone has fifty-five million and is the most densely
populated area in the whole world.

"One of the first books we printed in Indonesia was
What Christians Believe. In two months only 600 were
left from our first 3,000. Then on November 1st, after
our first edition had completely sold out we received an
order for 4,500 to be delivered in one month. Before I
showed it to Willard I said, 'You had better sit down
first.' I thought the shock might be too much for him!
The printer is a Christian and when we showed him the
order, he was enthusiastic and said, 'Even though we are
swamped, we will get the books out.' The Dutch Re-
formed Church in West Java was giving the book as a
Christmas present to their constituency! Who could have
asked for such a source of distribution?! No salesmanship
was used (we had never even visited them) no advertising;
while we were busy cooped up in our little corner the
Lord had done this for us. By 1961 18,000 copies of this
book had been printed. It is actually the Emmaus Bible
Correspondence Course put into book form.

"In the last four years we have published 142,000 books
in the Indonesian language, most of these have contained
over 120 pages. They have included twenty-three different
titles. Besides these, we have printed around 200,000
tracts and booklets, 8,000 wall mottoes in color, and many
Sunday school pictures and papers, and over 40,000 Scripture Text Calendars. This may sound like quite a lot
of literature, but in comparison to the great need it is very
little. Our present plans include a greatly stepped-up
program of actual publishing. As the Lord has so wonderfully enabled so far we know He is going to help and
provide as the work expands.

" 'What do you do other than selling books over the
counter?' some ask. Our work is not only selling books,
it is ministering to hungry souls. Another avenue of distribution is through conferences where book tables are

arranged. At first we carried the books to the conferences and sold them ourselves. I well remember the times I had to lug suitcases full of books on long bus rides over the mountains. Now most of this work is done by the churches. They tell us ahead of time where they are going to hold meetings, we ship the books to them and they take full responsibility for selling them.

"Sometimes one gets very tired. In a hot country all this means real hard work. We are the only group who distribute Chinese books in any large quantity all over Indonesia, and there are hundreds of thousands of Chinese in Indonesia. When we take books to their conferences, they almost mob us in their desire to get them. At the Malang Bible School there are sixty Chinese students. If they want a Bible dictionary or concordance in Chinese, they have to get it from us. It is so very worthwhile being able to help these young people in their study of the Word, providing them with literature they could not otherwise obtain. From that Bible school there are now eight students taking advanced studies in the U.S. In Indonesia there are fifteen different Bible schools and seminaries, under various missions or churches, who come to us for English books. They are overjoyed when they come into the store, and thank us for making the books available to them. Sometimes it is a trial when about thirty of them come into the store at one time and some who know where the stocks of hard-to-obtain English books are kept go right back into the storeroom and try to get some of them. Willard calls out, 'Keep them out front, keep them out front!'

"Then there are the part-time helpers the Lord has sent along. Two people just could not cope with the tremendous job of publishing and distribution now being done. We were just desperate for help, but the Lord had an answer. He spoke to a missionary from another mission and sent her down for two days a week, though it meant a two and one-half hour bus trip, and she even pays her own fare. She proofreads for us and helps in the store. Another was a Chinese man who could read English and told us, 'I never knew that you had so many irons in the fire.' He offered to proofread for us when his office job was finished, and it takes hours to proofread these books. Another one was John Capron, from W.E.C. He did a lot of extra work in getting manuscripts ready. Another missionary had been a window decorator in Australia. In a short while he prepares an attractive window display that makes the passers-by stop and look. The Lord knows that neither Willard nor I are artistically inclined!

"We also thank the Lord for all the nationals He has sent in from among the church people. When, for instance, we get in 10,000 Sunday school pictures or papers we don't have time to fold and count them, so each church takes a couple of suitcases full, and the women fold and count them into one-hundreds. At other times when we receive 150 packages through the mail in one day, someone always seems ready to come along and help unwrap and mark the books.

"We had 16,000 calendars at the port, held up by the Customs for three months. They would not release them as they wanted to count them as pictures and charge 200 per cent duty. And calendars have to come through on time. So what could we do? We prayed, we wrote, asking others to pray. The Lord heard and answered and, still in time, we received the permit for free entry. I tell you we praised the Lord. Recently we imported paper into Indonesia — 358 reams, enough to print about 70,000 books! He is the God with whom *all* things are possible. Another thing which calls for prayerful vigilance is regarding the safe arrival of shipments of books. In 1958 a law was passed against Chinese literature coming into the country. From then on every package mailed from Hong Kong to an individual in Indonesia was just sent back again. We prayed that the Lord would safeguard the many packages of literature which C.L.C. had on order. Again prayer was answered, and we safely received fifty packages a day from Hong Kong. We only had two packages returned, while we received hundreds without trouble.

"To help meet the need of little books for children we bought a supply of picture blanks from England and then had the story printed in Indonesia. At first it was a great problem to get good translations for children. We found that people tend to translate in grown-up language even though it is a children's book. On one occasion our problem was solved in quite a unique way and with very far-reaching results. A missionary was using one of these books in English in a little village where she had a Bible club for children. One of the children who came was a naughty boy who delighted in making trouble and disturbing the other children. He was such a trial that she was about ready to send him home and tell him not to come any more. In desperation she asked the Lord to show her some way to get his interest. Just then she thought of one of those books in English and brought it to him, saying, 'Harry, you are studying English now, would you like to take this book and read it and then put it into Indonesian?' Of course he thought she was giving him a pat on the back and recognizing how good he was in English. Several years later this boy, Harry, told me the story. 'Do you know,' he said, 'my first interest in Christianity came when I read that book of Old Testament stories.' Today that same boy has graduated from seminary and is an assistant pastor. He is also a very gifted choir director and song writer. He won first prize in all of Indonesia for a hymn which he had written.

"There are also the more 'indirect' ways of fellowship and service which the literature missionary is called upon to make in the outworking of his total ministry. On one occasion all the follow-up work in connection with the campaigns of an evangelist from the U.S. was turned over to us. Our job was to send out literature to all who had signed decision cards in each of the cities where campaigns had been held. These campaigns were supported by the national churches. without a penny coming from any foreign mission.

"Another thing that the Lord has used in Indonesia is the correspondence course ministry. These are produced by the Christian and Missionary Alliance and go out all over Indonesia. Because the demand is so great we have been able to assist the Alliance, sending out the courses to the people in our end of the island. This has given us an amazing contact with people. Anywhere you go now, on the bus or train someone will come up to you and tell you that they have taken the Light of Life Correspondence Course. This is particularly true when giving out tracts.

"In the uncertain atmosphere of national and international affairs faith is constantly tested in the matter of finances. Yet every test is but a further opportunity to see the God of miracles at work. Such was the case two years ago when within one-half hour the 1000 rupiah note became worth only 100 rupiahs. We had just bought fifty reams of paper and, in order to make the payment of 20,000 rupiahs, we had to literally scrape together everything we had. Willard dipped into personal monies and I gathered up all but twenty rupiahs from my purse. This sudden devaluation, without any prior warning, reduced us almost to our last penny. But God saw us through. If we had been counting only on C.L.C. at a time like that, the bottom could have fallen out of everything for us. It is in situations like this that we need to know that the Lord has sent us and that we are doing His work. Then we can also stand on the assurance that He has a way out.

"Folks can hardly believe that we run a literature work of this size and yet often have only about 200 rupiahs on hand. Our God is still the God of the impossible and He still never lets the barrel of meal become entirely empty.

It is wonderful to be part of a mission that really believes God and sees Him work miracles continually. May we never get so big that we lose our faith in our great God. Anyone, called of God, with a willing heart, a passion for souls, a package of books large or small, and faith in God, can be a C.L.C.er.

"The greatest reward of all in this literature ministry is to know that lives are being blessed. Every once in a while we are allowed a glimpse of the fruit of our labors. A young woman, who had been to Bible school and was now in the seminary in Djakarta, came to me. She had picked up an English book telling of a doctor who witnessed wherever he went. 'Why didn't anyone tell me about the responsibility of witnessing for Jesus?' she asked. She bought many more of these books and passed them around to her friends. Later we had the book translated and printed in Indonesian. It has been a great blessing. There are real possibilities here in Indonesia. We must pray for a Holy Ghost revival which will set the Christians on fire to witness. They don't know about witnessing to others."

Willard Stone shares these convictions and, in a recent letter he reported other instances of blessing and encouragement. "For sometime now a nineteen year old Javanese lad has been working at a store a few blocks from the bookshop. On his trips to deposit money in the bank he often stopped at the bookstore to browse around. During these visits he bought several of our translations of the Moody colportage books, and some others.

"One morning recently he came into the shop and asked to speak with me. He was actually trembling and his speech was almost incoherent. About all you could understand was that he had an overwhelming sense of sin and was seeking help. We made arrangements to meet at his older brother's house the following morning. There he showed me the books that he had been reading and again expressed concern over the sins in his life. We had some time together in the Scriptures and in prayer. Subsequently we had several more sessions together and he has come out with a definite public testimony for Christ. The lad told me that no one had spoken to him about his soul. His conviction came as a result of his reading and caused him to come to us for help. He still needs prayer. His Moslem brother and former friends are not sympathetic. Apparently he has tried to make restitution for past misdeeds and the person or persons involved think that he is crazy.

"Some weeks ago some Chinese friends were visiting the Roman Catholic hospital here in the city. They noticed a Dutchman there and stopped to chat with him because he looked so sad. They discovered that he spoke English fluently and asked us to give him an English New Testament. He was glad to have this as he said he had lots of time to read.

"This man, of Dutch descent, but an Indonesian citizen, formerly held a responsible position with a large firm here. He has had chronic lung trouble for years, which culminated in a bout with pneumonia some months ago. This knocked him right off his feet and his doctor had given him up as hopeless. His lungs have lost their elasticity and his heart is being overworked in the struggle to supply his body with vital oxygen.

"He received the Word of God gladly, though it was all new to him as he had not been a 'religious person.' The Chinese brothers also continued to visit and witness to him and prayed with him for his physical healing. He gives evidence of a deep repentance for sins and there is such a marked improvement in his physical condition that his doctor is releasing him from the hospital. He is to go to Malang, where it is cooler, for rest and observation.

"Last Saturday night as we talked of the Lord's grace he was just weeping because of wrongs done to others years ago. But as we left he was beaming with joy at what the Lord has done for him, and that we would not be visiting him in the hospital anymore. He expects to be released this week.

"A few days ago we received a letter from a young graduate of Teacher's School in northern Sulawesi. He said that he had just read the translation of Oswald Smith's *Passion for Souls*. He says that it has set his heart aflame and he feels the call of God to preach the gospel. He wants to give himself to the Lord's service and desires Bible training to that end. Praise God. This is what we want to see, of course—these men getting a burden to get the gospel to their own people."

23

JAPAN—NATION OF LITERATES

Everybody knows certain facts about Japan. A population of ninety-six million people make these the most crowded islands in the world (rivaled only by Java). Industrially and economically it is the most dynamic and go-ahead nation of the East. Though wide open to the Christian missionary and Christian message, it is desperately slow in response in contrast to the Chinese who so readily receive the Word.

The challenge of Japan to C.L.C. came directly to Ken Adams in the U.S.A. in 1949. General MacArthur had issued his challenge to the West for thousands of missionaries. Its high rate of literacy made an obvious appeal to a literature crusade, but in a sense the final operative word came from another literature mission, and from another Ken—Ken Taylor, who had recently been appointed director of Moody Press. When the two Kens met there was an immediate affinity in spirit. They talked of the new horizon of an extended world outreach, recognized the significant place of literature and shared a common desire to help meet the growing opportunity. As they parted Ken Taylor remarked, "If C.L.C. is interested in developing in Japan, let me know, because I think Moody would like to help in some way." This was the second offer of help by Moody to C.L.C. and has expanded since into their actively helping in other places such as Indonesia and the West Indies. This may be God's way of giving back (with interest) the first gift given by C. T. Studd to D. L. Moody in 1885, with which Moody told him he was going to start building the Bible School in Chicago.

The decision made, Ken Adams visited Japan and met in conference with the leaders of fifteen missionary societies and a number of Japanese brethren. All urged C.L.C. to come to Japan as quickly as possible. Ken accepted the challenge and indeed had his eyes on a large building which he hoped might become a literature center and headquarters for missionary activities. This did not eventuate. We were to find that God's starts are usually small, becoming big rather than the other way around; that "no flesh should glory in His presence." But the vision and commission became clear and was right, and has remained so until today.

The actual start was made in 1950 by Ray Oram from England. "As a result of the visit of Ken Adams to Japan," says Ray, "I had introductions to a number of key people. One was a wonderful Japanese pastor, David Tsutada, often called the John Wesley of Japan. He had emerged from prison at the end of the war broken in health and penniless; but God had laid His hand upon him, and from nothing a work of God had been raised up which today stretches over much of the country. Crowds of students flocked to his Sunday services. I would sit in the meetings recognizing the power and authority in his ministry, though not understanding a word, while he preached for an hour and more.

"Pastor Tsutada became a great friend and I came to rely on his advice. Early in 1951 he spoke to me about a Japanese Christian, one of his members, who wished to serve the Lord and suggested that he might be God's man for C.L.C. I met Kawai-san and heard his story."

Kawai had been in the Japanese Army in the Philippines. Only ten of the five hundred men of his unit survived the rigors of campaigning in the jungles; but promises he made to God in times of peril were forgotten on his return, when he sought to make his fortune in the shoe business. Fortunately for him, it failed, and it was God's recalling voice to him. He spent three months in prayer and seeking the Lord, until the word came to him to "stand up," his prayer was heard and his praying should end.

To join Ray in Christian literature work was attractive enough, but the life of faith was something he could not easily understand or accept. To step out in the Lord's service, trusting His promises and with no visible means of support, was something he had not heard of before nor seen lived out. What was more, he had a family of four. But the Scriptures he had been given during his time with God—Galatians 1:1 and I Corinthians 2:9—held him, and in 1951 he and his wife joined Ray in C.L.C.

His first days with the Crusade were not without murmurings for which he had to constantly seek God's forgiveness. "God brought Kawai-san into the work at a time of extreme weakness," recalls Ray, "when many of the things we did must have looked foolish in the eyes of a Japanese. What a blessing he has been to the work. In his love for the Lord he was willing to undergo privation and great difficulties for the cause of Christ." One problem was the language. Ray knew almost no Japanese and Kawai very little English. They often had to resort to drawing pictures or gesticulating with their hands; but they found that prayer cleared the atmosphere even though each prayed in his own language. Differences of temperament and points of view due to the wide divergence in culture, coupled with attractive business offers and the advice of friends, often pulled hard at Kawai; but the same word of the Lord always held him.

"Another of Pastor Tsutada's generous actions was to offer the use of part of his church office in downtown Tokyo for a small bookstore," continues Ray. "The office was on the third floor and many were the hundreds of book parcels we carried up those stairs. Soon shelves were rigged up and books displayed—I can still see the look of wonder and awe on the faces of the Japanese Christians as they handled the English books and realized these were Christian publications. It would be a long time before such were available in their language."

From there they moved nearer to where Kawai was living, to a room in a Christian hospital. Even this move would have made Sanballat laugh, much as he did over Nehemiah's earlier efforts. With no money and no truck they moved everything in twenty cases, taking three hours by elevated train, and annoying the conductor when they had to change with all that baggage.

The need for central living quarters became acute with the prospect of increased staff, both foreign and national. Ray had by now married Margaret Findlayson, and this led them to seek and locate a good-sized house in Ichikawa, a suburb of Tokyo. This served the work well for eight years. For the move this time they had a second-hand army jeep. But even with this they ran into trouble. It was so old that it would "run and stop," until finally it stopped to move no more! The two men had to push the jeep through the snow for the last part of the journey, and through an area where Kawai used to live.

It took time to come to a clear understanding regarding the type of literature program best suited for C.L.C. in Japan. Lessons were naturally learned by trial and error. Should it be publishing, bookstores, bookmobiles, importing of English books, or what? A first attempt was made at publishing by the production of a concordance in Japanese, but if it was not an actual flop, it was "no howling success." An experiment was made in getting Christian books to secular bookstores in the fifty main cities of Japan, but this was not too successful either. Many of the managers were not Christians and were more interested in secular lines which had a better market.

A bookstall at the Tokyo Gospel Hour among the

hundreds of American servicemen proved to be a very useful ministry. "What a thrill it was to see them buying books," recalls Ray, "good solid study books, some of the finest devotional material, inspirational literature that was sure to bless. I especially wondered how the sailors managed to cram all they bought into their small lockers, but they came again and again and told in glowing terms of the help the books had been to them."

That bookstores were the C.L.C.'s best ministry took clear shape when Miss Irene Webster-Smith, one of the oldest missionaries in Japan, known and loved by all, built a student center in a strategic location in Tokyo, in an area where there are twelve colleges and 300,000 students. She incorporated a bookstore in this building and, being a great friend to C.L.C., asked the Crusade to take it over. This set us at the heart of things in Tokyo though, even so, there was insufficient room for bulk storage and mail order. More recently, because of an enlargement of the building and the bookstore, we have been able to greatly expand the general ministry, having the offices, mail order and bookstore all in one building. Undoubtedly, the initial move into this fine location has proved to be the most significant factor in the developing of the nation-wide ministry.

"The first summer in Japan a visit was made to Karuizawa," continues Ray. "This is a hill resort where many of the missionaries and others gather each year for times of refreshing, both spiritual and physical. We took with us many boxes of English books and, with permission, set up a booktable in the conference hall. Before and after each meeting the missionaries would crowd around the table, thrilled to see so many books that could be of help to them in their own lives and in the work of God. It was a common sight to see these Christian workers leaving the conference hall with a load of books under their arms.

"Seeing the hunger for good Christian literature brought

home the need of a summer store in Karuizawa. Through the kindness of Japanese Christians we were able to rent a half-store on the main street, stocking it with English and Japanese literature. We were thus able to minister to the crowds of Japanese who, in increasing numbers, held conferences there and were delighted to find the Christian bookstore. It became the meeting place for many and in the afternoons they would be found browsing among the books. One summer a girl of about twelve years, the daughter of missionaries, came in daily to read one of the books. Alas—before it could be finished her family returned to their work; but the next year she was back to finish it."

Sendai, a city of 400,000, situated towards the north on the main island of Honshu, was the first to have a provincial C.L.C. bookstore. This was "manned" by a young Japanese woman, Sato Ukiko-san. It was opened at the suggestion of Pastor Tsutada, following a successful evangelistic campaign in the city, and is in a good location close to the university.

Further north, on the island of Hokkaido is Sapporo, the capital city, and this early became an objective of C.L.C. Japan. Premises were secured and a start was made in 1954, but in 1961 a move was made into a much more central location in the heart of the city. The ministry continues to flourish. The store is the only one of its kind on the island and its services and ministry are reaching into every corner of this northern territory.

From the very beginning help and encouragement were given to the C.L.C. by W.E.C. missionaries working in rural Japan. Bob and Dorothy Gerry went to Japan as W.E.C. workers, and after being loaned to C.L.C. for a time to help fill an urgent need, they felt convinced of a personal call to literature work. When Ray Oram, who had begun the work in Japan, responded to the call to open the work in the Philippine Islands, Bob Gerry became the C.L.C. leader in Japan.

Bob and Dorothy first served with C.L.C. in the Kyoto center, located in a busy section of this historic city of central Honshu. The property became ours by the usual "unusual" provision of God. After searching around, Bob and Ray were directed to a boarded-up place which had not been used since the war. They squeezed their way in and liked the building despite its run-down appearance. Arriving back they reported to the others, saying that the place "had possibilities"—the phrase which has become a catchword in C.L.C. The next day they looked it over again and liked it still more. The conviction grew that this was God's place for the Crusade. But could it be obtained without the usual red tape so common in buying properties? Before they left the building they prayed and declared their faith that God would provide and perform another of His miracles. Going outside, they saw a couple on the opposite side of the road staring at them. It looked like trouble. Bob and Ray walked on ahead. But when the Japanese interpreter came out of the building, the couple tackled him. Who were they but the owners who lived in a remote part of the town and "happened" to be in the area visiting his mother. While in the district, they decided to walk by their property—but for no particular reason! Result? The owners were intrigued, not offended, and invited them to their home, entertaining them to the favorite Japanese dish of ofushi (raw fish). Then they were ready to talk business and arrived at an agreeable price for the building and land. To complete the transaction about half the price was needed immediately. W.E.C. had money available which they gladly donated and the deal was closed. Thank God there has been some lasting fruit as a result of this literature ministry in Kyoto. One of the evidences is that three of the Japanese workers, later to join the Crusade, came through their contact with this center.

Hiroshima, famous for its tragic war history as the first city to experience the atom bomb, is a most strategically located city in the south on the main island of Honshu. Helped by a generous gift from the Back to the Bible Broadcast, a book center was opened in this city of 350,000. The results were most encouraging at first, but then things slumped and it looked as though the work might have to close down. But faith persisted and, under the fine leadership of Kawai-san and his wife, the work is now stronger than at any previous time and there is evidence of much blessing. Hiroshima is also the gateway to a conglomeration of 2,000 islands in the Inland Sea between the islands of Honshu and Shikoku, the majority of which are inhabited by people cut off from the main stream of Japanese life and yet almost totally literate. Several preliminary trips have been made to a few of these islands but extra workers will be needed before these can be reached in a more adequate way.

The seventh C.L.C. book center is in Okayama, a port midway between Hiroshima and Kobe from which travelers cross to the island of Shikoku. It was opened as a result of an urgent invitation from the Swedish Covenant Mission who also helped financially at the start. It was a launch of faith in a particular sense because, as Ken Cullen said, "At the time we agreed to go, there were no workers, no money, no nothing, nor any prospects. Yet within six weeks of taking this step we had six Japanese applicants, so that within five months there were seven new workers—six national and one foreign. Some of the C.L.C. team, nationals and foreigners, have joined the Swedish workers in caravan evangelism in the many villages around Okayama, using a van with a loud-speaker and visiting the houses with tracts and books. Children come in plenty, but adults have been more reserved as in all the country areas of Japan, twenty being an average attendance. Many have bought books at a nickel apiece. In one village we found a lady who spoke broken English, which was evidently rusty with non-use. In her younger days she had attended a Christian university. She was so thrilled and moved to hear the old-time message that she wept and prayed for forgiveness and restoration. She had been seeking the Lord for all those intervening years and had found Him at last. Regular meetings are now held in her village home."

The C.L.C. team in Japan now number twenty-two—nine foreigners and thirteen Japanese. It has not been easy for the Japanese, because not many can see the literature calling as a lifetime commission. They tend to feel that they are not really serving the Lord unless they are pastors or evangelists. Concerning the Lord's provision for the Japanese members of the team, Bob Gerry says, "somewhat recently in the history of the work, we have been using a one-pool sharing system of support. It is not exactly an equal share, but nearly so, of all that is received by the foreign and national missionaries. The Lord has wonderfully supplied, especially in the last two or three years, under this system. As a result we have seen the Japanese receive at least a minimum adequate amount of money for their monthly support. We never think in terms of accepting or not accepting a Japanese worker on the basis of the money that is available. Rather, we see the need, consider the suitability of the applicant, and then trust the Lord to supply what is needed for the support of those additional workers."

How we thank God for the steady increase of the work over the years. The sales doubled in 1961 and they are climbing noticeably higher in 1962. "In one way sales are only a small factor of the total work," says Bob, "yet they are important. They do represent an increasing volume of literature going out. This is of primary importance. Yet we do not want to put undue emphasis on sales. Our first concern is that souls are being touched and won for the Lord.

"I would like to emphasize the importance of literature in Japan and its place in evangelistic work. Let me repeat: Japan is the world's most literate country. Estimates vary slightly, but it is safe to say that 99 per cent of the Japanese people are literate. When you ride on the subways and trains you see many, many people redeeming the time by reading magazines, books and newspapers. Unfortunately you don't see them reading Bibles and Christian literature in the same way. A large percentage of the literature they read is not edifying. It is, in many cases, immoral. There is an abundance of Communistic literature to be had and the Communist influence through literature is as great as ever.

"There are some 10,000 bookstores scattered throughout Japan, yet we are probably safe in saying there are not more than thirty full-time Christian bookstores in the country. The opportunity of the Christian bookstore is tremendous, especially if the people serving in the store are really burdened for souls and are deeply convinced of what can be done through getting Christian literature to people. For instance: many people come into our Tokyo bookstore; some out of curiosity, others to buy Christmas cards or for some quite superficial reason—yet they can all be witnessed to. A tract put in the parcel they purchase is a further means of witness. There are many people who come in off the street to our bookstore who would not go into a meeting at the Student Christian Center next door. We often have as many non-Christians drop into the bookstore in one day as would attend an evangelistic rally at the Center. On the other hand, we are able to introduce many of those coming into the store to the Center and to its activities, and in that way assist the evangelistic program.

"But much remains to be done. There are probably some 600 cities in Japan with a population of 10,000 or more, that have no gospel witness, no church, no evangelist and no Christian bookstore. To us this shows the importance of literature. It can be sent into areas where there is no church and no permanent witness. It is our hope and intention to get many more bookstores established and a more extensive literature program developed. And not only to open C.L.C. bookstores but also to encourage other missions and missionaries in their literature ministries so that much more can be done throughout Japan. The doors are wide open."

24

STILL FURTHER AFIELD

When Ida Howlett left England in 1951 to start literature work in India, not many were enthusiastic. A single woman to open up C.L.C. in so vast a country?! Some openly expressed doubt of the wisdom of it. On the other hand there was strong conviction among the leaders that God's time had come for India and that, as the Lord had commissioned a worker, He had the plan in view. On arrival in India, Ida went first to the W. E. C. Headquarters in Fatehpur, North India, to grapple with the language.

In Madras, South India, the other half of God's plan was taking shape. Donald David, an Indian brother, had been operating a bookroom in the city for seven years, which he called Evangelical Literature Service. He did not know why he took up literature work except that the call came after a period of many years of trial and disappointment, which had fixed his heart on God. Phil Booth, the C.L.C. Foreign Secretary in London, had heard of Donald and his E.L.S., and a letter of invitation from Phil brought him to London. The world vision of C.L.C., combined with what he saw of how little becomes much when God is in it and the word of faith spoken and acted upon, brought Donald to the decision that he should join his E.L.S. to C.L.C.; for, as he said, "In an atmosphere of faith it is easy to get a vision of the tremendous resources of God which are available to those who dare to stake all on Him." The word Donald had from God was that by so doing he would see a repetition in India of the miracle of the feeding of the five thousand through an expanded literature ministry.

In 1954, when Phil Booth visited India, E.L.S. was registered with the government as an Indian literature mission, an indigenous organization, retaining for convenience its name of Evangelical Literature Service.

During Phil's visit the C.L.C. in north and south India were also united in another way. As Donald puts it, "Oneness of vision and burden for the work to which God had called Ida and me finally culminated in the happy bonds of marriage." Happy, and blessed also, for C.L.C. India has steadily progressed since then, and the promise of the miracle of the five thousand is being fulfilled. "During the past seven years," says Donald, "we have watched Him providing the 'bread of life' to India's hungry millions. To meet the need of 400 million people speaking thirteen major languages is not humanly possible for any one organization. But God has been feeding some through our eight book centers opened through the years."

In obtaining their main shop and headquarters in Madras they had a lesson to learn. "Within two years our premises were totally inadequate for our needs," Donald continues. "Just a furlong away was a building strategically located and ideal for us. Convinced that God would have us claim this by faith we united in prayer for it. Nearly three years went by and still there was no sign of the building becoming vacant, so I am afraid we weakened in our stand of faith and rented another building. Six months later God enabled us to secure the former premises! He showed us how weak our faith had been and how little our patience. The hasty step became our 'Ishmael,' and for many years was a thorn in our sides. I trust we learned our lesson not to go ahead of the Lord!"

A second shop in Madras—the only city where C.L.C. has two shops—came through a friend, the Rev. Cyril

Thompson, Chaplain of Christ Church. "Asked if we would operate a second shop in Madras, we unhesitatingly said that we would," Donald recalls.

" 'Then you may have the new premises we have built on Mount Road for this purpose,' said Cyril Thompson. (This area to Madras is what Fifth Avenue is to New York, or Oxford Street is to London.) And it's just like the Lord to do the exceeding abundantly—He put it into the hearts of the Christ Church Committee to let us have the premises *rent free!*

"Our first branch bookstore was opened in Mussoorie (North India) in 1956, taking the store over from the Mussoorie Book Society. This was followed by the opening of Ootacamund and Kodaikanal in the south in 1957. These centers cater to thousands of visitors, particularly during the summer and autumn when these hill stations are most popular. The Lord sends into the shops people from all parts of the country whom we would otherwise never meet, and how great is our joy to hear of souls being blessed through the literature that goes out. A special feature of our ministry is to provide bookstalls for Keswick-type missionary conventions. This service is much appreciated for by and large, missionaries serve in remote areas and therefore look forward to making annual purchases at these conventions. Incidentally, our book center at Ootacamund is located in the premises of the church where C. T. Studd was a pastor during his short term in India.

"Our Bangalore (south) and Lucknow (north) centers were opened in 1960 and 1961. In these cities the potential for literature evangelism is very great. The former is the most industrialized city in South India, and because of its pleasant, moderate climate affords many privileges which are being sought after by a continuous stream of settlers. Lucknow, in many ways, is the counterpart of Bangalore in the north of India. A special feature of our work in this city is to conduct, almost non-stop throughout the year, bookstalls in the various schools and colleges, of which there are not a few. It is a wonderful ministry to sow the seed of the Word of God into the fertile minds of India's future generation.

"The famous Christian Medical College and Hospital in Vellore is considered one of the finest institutions of its kind in South East Asia. For a long time it was our prayer that God would open the door for us to supply them with literature, and in 1960 our prayer was answered. Imagine our great joy, one day, when the General Superintendent of the hospital walked into our headquarters in Madras and said, 'Why do we not have in Vellore the type of material you stock here?'

" 'We would be glad to help you in every way possible,' was the reply, little expecting what was to follow!

" 'Then will you come tomorrow and take complete management of the shop in our hospital?'

"We were able to respond to this request and now are in Vellore seeking to provide healing for the souls of those who come to have their bodies treated. In nearly every phase of the institution's multitudinous activities we are given a part for which we praise God. Who can tell how many we shall meet on that 'great day' whom we have indirectly brought nearer the great Physician?

"The gift of a bookmobile for long tours, especially in the Rajastan area, and for the encouragement of Christians in isolated places, has been a great help.

"As an indigenous mission it is not surprising that in our team of workers nationals far exceed the number of foreigners. God has called them (now numbering thirteen) from being businessmen, teachers and government employees, with their varying talents, into fullest fellowship as a missionary team. God has moulded us into a happy fellowship of which He is the Head.

"There are also the trials and testings. Our 'faith' principle of working gets severely tested. In a literature mission where we adopt normal business practices of

buying and selling, earning a profit which is used for
furthering our objectives, the church in India does not
feel a special obligation to support such workers with
gifts. When we have been severely tested, Philippians
4:19 has still been valid: 'But my God shall supply all
your need according to his riches in glory by Christ
Jesus.' The rapid opening of new centers has often
stretched our finances to the breaking point, but deliverance has always arrived in time."

Despite this, the Indian E.L.S. (C.L.C.), under its
national leadership, has taken a striking stand on faith
principles. Up to the beginning of 1962 the principle had
been what the national workers have recorded in these
words: "We thank God for the vision given to E.L.S.
from the very inception of the mission to look to Him
alone for the supply of all needs. It was C.L.C.'s faith
challenge that brought to birth E.L.S.! As far as we know,
no other literature mission operates as we do on a basis
of equality between nationals and missionaries even to the
extent of pooling finances. This has been a unique stand,
and well-pleasing to God."

At their recent Workers' Conference a change to a
separate national workers' fund and a missionary fund
was agreed to. National missionaries will now share equally what God supplies each month and foreign missionaries
will do likewise with their funds unless they decide otherwise. Their bold and solid reason for this is that, as the
conference report reads: "Our national brethren recommend that they come out of the general pool and accept
only what money is sent to them, the missionaries deciding
among themselves how their allowances are to be divided.
We want to make it a matter of prayer and faith *that the
Lord will raise up those within the national church to
give.*"

We think this is a splendid indication of the uprising
of the Spirit of God in the national churches, stirring
them to see Him not only call out the national workers,

but also to supply all their financial needs through national resources. In this new missionary age, they are surely pointing the way and leading the way which others will follow.

What of the future? In summary Donald David says, "We believe God is giving India a special opportunity to hear of His full salvation through our Lord Jesus Christ. Government reports declare 40 per cent of the population to be literate, and with the present literacy drive millions will become literate each year. What a potential for literature evangelism!"

A letter from a literature conference, held in Pakistan in 1959, made a direct appeal to C.L.C. to start work in that country. The conference was attended by seventy five missionaries of seventeen different missions. The conference secretary, Vern Rock, wrote: "I have been instructed by the conference to extend to your organization a request to consider the advisability of opening a bookshop in Karachi, and later near the new capital city. Such an undertaking would receive the gratitude and patronage of the Christian community in Pakistan and definitely help in the evangelization of this Moslem land."

Both Donald David, representing the Evangelical Literature Service (C.L.C.) in India, and Ken Adams for the home bases, wrote accepting the invitation as a challenge for which they would ask the Lord to provide the workers. Two W.E.C. missionaries on furlough from Pakistan, Miles and Beryl Sim, had seen the significance of literature when on the field and were seeking the Lord about it. When the news came of this call from all the missions, it was the Lord's word to them. They are now in Karachi, Pakistan's largest city, with a new recruit, Clara Bort. A doctor and his wife from California, who heard of the new opportunities in literature evangelism through Rev. Carl Tanis, indicated they would like to help establish a bookstore. The need in Pakistan was presented to them, and they personally donated $5,000 for this new book center. As Ken Adams says, "This is one of the rare occasions when we have gone to a new field with sufficient funds actually in hand to do the job. It's a nice feeling."

Bertram Jones, a former director of a shoe manufacturing company, and his wife, Margaret, were the C.L.C. pioneers in Latin America. They established the first center in Montevideo, the capital of Uruguay, assisted by Doris Whybrow (now Mrs. Race), the daughter of the Whybrows of Ludgate Hill. It was hard and slow going because, although Latin America is one of the great harvest fields of the world today and is experiencing almost a twentieth century reformation, Uruguay is not so responsive. At one time the question even arose about the advisability of closing down or handing over to another agency. It was one of those crisis moments when a work seems to hang by a thread; but at the home base, as they went to prayer, God gave faith not only to hold on but that this same center would become a springboard for advance.

A young couple, Jack and Rachel Roeda, took over in 1955 from the two veterans. They made it one of their first objectives to put bookstands in each of the churches throughout the country. Within a year or so several trips had been undertaken. Using buses and other means of local transportation, wide sections of the country were visited. These personal visits to the pastors, informing them that C.L.C. had come as guests of the national churches to serve them with literature, encouraged many to see their people's need of literature and started a flow of good books throughout the country.

Leaving the book center with Gladys Brownlee, Jack raised his eyes to wider horizons. Gladys, in spite of the effects of a childhood polio attack and often in temperatures that greatly tired her, became the mainstay of the

Montevideo work. Enlisting various national workers, and despite financial pressures which made it barely possible to carry on the existing work, Jack responded to a call to Mar del Plata, a resort city on Argentina's Atlantic Coast, to which more than a million people go each summer for their vacation. Friends in Argentina had appealed to C.L.C. to cooperate with them in this venture and help get a bookstore opened for the vacation season. This was accomplished and the response was most encouraging. Finding so many open hearts the store became a permanency in the hands of national workers, Jake and Kathleen Kraay, and provided literature to the churches over a wide area.

Capable national workers, as in the West Indies, Japan and India, have been the key to the C.L.C. in Latin America—the task of the missionaries gradually becoming more to coordinate the work. The start in Mar del Plata led, in due course, to what has always been the primary objective in Latin America, the great city of Buenos Aires, Argentina's capital with a seven million population. A national couple, Jose and Norma Wojnorawicz, built up a stock of books in their home in anticipation of a bookstore in a good location. Prices were high and out of reach. Meanwhile, with his bookmobile, Jose visited many churches and persuaded them to buy books for their libraries. Then came an opportunity to purchase a store in a good shopping area for $9,000, necessitating a $4,000 down payment. While on furlough Jack Roeda received about $2,000 for this project; then two groups in the U.S.A., the Back to the Bible Broadcast and the Moody Literature Mission, both contributed $2,000 and the Center was taken.

Chile was opened by the zeal of national Christians, Arnaldo Umana and his wife, who first worked as colporteurs with the C.L.C., and then opened a small store in the port of Talcahuano, near the city of Conception. More recently Jack and Rachel Roeda on returning from furlough, have taken on responsibility for a second store located in Chile's capital, Santiago. "In such countries as Chile," says Jack, "the evangelical cause is going forward by leaps and bounds. It is said that Latin America, of all the continents in the world, is perhaps the one most open to the gospel and we praise God that this is so. People who have been for many years depressed and deceived by the claims of the Roman church are now open to the claims of Jesus Christ. But, of course, we also know that satan is entrenched, and this calls for a greater effort on the part of all Christians here to reach out to their own people with the gospel. In these days of growing nationalism we missionaries feel especially privileged that we can put this weapon of evangelism, the powerful printed page, into the hands of the national Christians.

"In these few short years we have seen the C.L.C. ministry branch out into several South American countries and have a tremendous ministry to the churches and the unsaved. With the meager resources we have had in the natural, we can only praise God for what has been wrought in bringing living literature to these who, for so many centuries, have been held in the chains of Roman Catholic darkness. Latin America is known as a Catholic continent, yet we have found hungry hearts in many of these countries, and most of the Catholics are Catholics in name only. Because of this vacuum, our literature ministry has a wonderful opportunity to contact these uncommitted people and to bring them the glorious light of the gospel that can change their lives and give them the purpose in life so many thousands lack.

"In this work we face many false cults and the ever-present danger of Communism. Each day the newsstands are spreading the poison of the Communist doctrine and it grieves us to see that the people, because of their needs and the economic conditions that prevail, often feel that some change, any change, will be for the better. It is a problem. All around us we see poverty and whole classes of people who have no hope in this world. Yet we hate to see them deceived by the materialistic approach of the Communists. But in Chile we have found many open hearts for the gospel, and there is an openness we have never experienced in other contacts with the peoples of Latin America."

Brazil, with the reputation of having the fastest-growing Protestant church in the world, has been an obvious C.L.C. target for years. A visit by Ken Adams, during which he received much encouragement from David Glass (experienced literature missionary of the Evangelical Union of South America); a survey trip into southern Brazil by Jim Finlay (W.E.C. pioneer in Uruguay); and finally a visit by Jack Roeda, led to action. Jack found a great spiritual hunger in Brazil. He reports: "The Lord is doing a mighty work there, and literature is playing a key role in this over-all evangelistic outreach. Through the survey trips we made the Lord burdened our hearts for the large city of Porto Alegre. There were certain denominational bookstores, but no key interdenominational store to serve the public in the downtown area. God put this city upon our hearts and in a wonderful way we saw personnel supplied as Tom and Lily Mc-Clelland took over the work and were later joined by Roland Jennings."

Tom and Lily were W.E.C. missionaries in neighboring Uruguay when the literature call became clear to them. In 1958 they had the usual start: "The thing that stands out most," says Tom, "is the miraculous way the Lord brought us through the multitude of difficulties that barred the way. We faced difficulties of inexperience; neither Lily nor I had extensive training for a literature ministry. We had language difficulties; within months of entering the country we were engaged full time in the work. We encountered financial difficulties that at times nearly crushed the ministry out of existence. There were also difficulties of a physical nature; I was laid up in the hospital within a few months of opening the store. Someone has said that when God wants to work a miracle, He starts with a difficulty; and certainly we have seen the Lord's deliverance by a series of miracles, and we praise Him for rolling all our burdens away.

"How does one start a Christian bookstore without any previous training?" continues Tom. "The first thing, obviously, was location. Joshua and the children of Israel had to walk around Jericho for seven days. I don't know if Porto Alegre was any harder than Jericho, but Jack Roeda and I had to walk round and round the central streets for a month before we found a suitable location for our bookstore! It was on the fifth floor of a modern, downtown building. Not exactly what we wanted; but the Lord gave us peace that it was His choice for the opening of the work in Brazil. In the three years since that modest beginning the effectiveness of a literature ministry has been amply demonstrated. Tons of gospel literature, Bibles, books, tracts, records and other items have been distributed effectively, and missionaries and national pastors have come to depend upon us for their literature needs." Three years later the move was made to a ground-floor location right in the center of town, a block and a-half from the main commercial street. When the move was completed it was, as Tom says, "a well-stocked, modern and attractive store." This is only regarded as a jumping-off point. The goal is a national literature crusade consisting of Brazilian and foreign personnel.

The spiritual needs in the interior of the state also concerned them. Trips were taken, but under difficulties. As Roland Jennings, who is concentrating on the mobile work, says, "Packing a couple of suitcases and boxes with books, traveling by bus and staying in a place until the stock was exhausted was strenuous work. We had calls and appeals from the interior as people constantly wrote in wanting literature and inquiring as to when we were going to visit them. All this was most encouraging and we saw big possibilities in this type of work, and so were constrained to pray for a suitable vehicle."

One or two gifts encouraged them and the final deliverance came through the Christian Life Mission of Wheaton, Illinois, who sent a gift of $3,000. "With the Volkswagen bookmobile," says Roland, "we have been able to visit many large towns in the state during the past year. Tons of books and Bibles have been sold. When one starts off now on a literature trip it is no longer a couple of suitcases, but a well-loaded van with anything up to half-ton of goods. Many of the roads in the interior are not too suitable for vehicles. Some are impassable in the wet season. Often one has to resort to putting on chains to get through the mud. On a recent trip it was through floods. When just about past the worst of it, we hit a rather deep patch which smothered the engine. We had to get the help of some young men to pull us onto dry land. After about half an hour of drying the wires and plugs, the motor eventually decided to start. The next town was forty miles ahead. It took three hours and we passed many vehicles stranded in the mire. When the hot weather comes, it's different, as the roads turn to sand and dust.

"You may ask, 'Why do you spend all this time and energy traveling for days to these places?' If you could see the welcome we get in most places, the appreciation shown and the way people purchase the literature, you would understand. We also see around us on every hand the devil's agents spreading their hellish literature. Next to Communism, I would say that Spiritism is the biggest enemy of the cross in Brazil. Their publishing and distribution program is colossal compared with the united evangelical effort. Catholicism, too, is on the march with the printed page and doing all she can to keep her hold on the people. Our best seller at the book fairs is always the Bible. We carry the one published by the Catholics as well as the one by the Bible Society. The Catholic one sells for 400 crusarios; the evangelical one for 150; so you know which one sells better! In this way hundreds of Bibles have been carried away by unsaved people."

25

OPPORTUNITIES UNLIMITED

Without doubt God gives some people a nose for literature—"quick of scent" as Isaiah says. Robert and Muriel Sjoblom were missionaries of the Christian and Missionary Alliance and served in both China and Thailand. The thought of a street-front shop in Bangkok stirred their imagination, and in other ways the literature vision grew until an old copy of *Floodtide* came into Bob's hands and he remarked, "That's the vision I have for literature! I like to work with folks who have the same vision." That great missionary agency, one of the world's greatest and most spiritual, the Christian and Missionary Alliance do plenty in literature themselves, but Bob was feeling the call to an exclusive literature ministry which would ultimately serve all Thailand. Therefore is was graciously agreed that they should transfer to C.L.C., and they were accordingly released.

After a period at Fort Washington they set out for the field again in 1958. They then had the usual ladder-climbing process which seems to be the norm in opening a C.L.C. field. The search for property began and they found a low-priced house in a dead-end lane. From here literature began to flow out although they had already been selling books from the missionary guest house before they got that far.

Then followed the hunt for a shop location in high-priced Bangkok where they came upon an old building in the Pratunam market area. Bob had baptized the wife of the owner during his first year in Thailand! Ultimately a gift from the U.S.A. made possible the renting of half the downstairs and all the upstairs of this building.

They soon came up against the ways of the Oriental (and not only the Oriental!) business world. "We found that there were many ways to avoid the law," says Bob, "and had been offered the 'know-how' by friends and acquaintances, who were quite surprised that we were not interested in avoiding the law but in running a straight business for the Lord! At one time when paying our monthly tax the official remarked, 'You are too honest'!"

They had trouble with the building. "It was the rainy season and often the office floor was flooded. The open drain became the runway of rats, and our book cupboards were ideal nesting places. Once we had a manuscript on the desk and I discovered one morning that most of it was gone. After hunting about we came to the conclusion that the rats must have helped themselves. Later this proved true when a raid was made on them."

However, things improved as they got permission to raise the floor and develop an area behind the store. October 24, 1959 was the official opening day. From the first monthly sales reckoned in tens of dollars, they are now in hundreds, averaging $700 a month—a steady increase, though by no means large enough yet to make the work self-supporting.

The ministry has had to be three-fold—for the Thais, the main objective, but at present there is only a little evangelical literature available; for the Chinese, who control much of the business of the country; and for the foreigners, few in number but appreciative of the book ministry. To meet these needs a staff has gradually been built, an international team of four couples—one each from Australia, China, Thailand and the U.S.A.

As usual, it hasn't been easy for the national brethren to accept the "faith" standard. "Our Thai helper, Bun

Jope," explains Bob, "was willing to try it on a temporary basis. We even paid him a little amount the first three months, telling him that he would have to decide after that regarding this other method and whether or not he would stay. We felt that this was the only way that he would be able to understand what the work involved and how we lived. Perhaps this was a wrong way to do it, but at least he would not be staying with us without understanding what he would be getting into.

"For a team of workers to be called of God out of widely varying backgrounds into a close fellowship and ministry together is surely God's doing, not man's. It was never done before in Thailand. To be sure, there are problems and much to be learned by all. But our sufficiency in all this is of God. With this 'mixed' team we can reach our varied customers more satisfactorily. At all our booktables we find it best to have a Chinese looking after the Chinese table, a Thai at the Thai table, and a missionary (or at least someone who speaks English) at the English-language table. And sometimes the folk in the office feel they are 'seeing triple' after a session at adding long columns of figures without an adding machine, keeping inventory cards straight in makeshift paper cartons, or packing parcels on the small corner of a homemade table which is concurrently being used as a desk by someone else!"

It is always the hope of C.L.C. workers to improve premises or location whenever necessary and therefore a watchful eye is kept on any new buildings or vacated premises. So for the team in Thailand it was a happy day when, through the kind cooperation of a local Christian businessman, they were able to move into a fine modern building in one of the main areas of the city. The dedication was held on February 17, 1962 with representatives of several missions and local churches participating.

The vision remains for the up-country areas. The future is bright with possibilities. They have a truck which is useful for getting the literature to booktables and local markets, but their further aims are to establish reading rooms in big towns in the provinces, and to have a book-mobile operating in rural areas in the same way as well-stocked mobiles go around with their drygoods or drug-store materials.

In Korea a start was made in 1956 by Timothy Ree, a Korean, and things seemed to get off to a good begin-ning. But this was not maintained, and in 1960 we had to close down this field—the only time this has happened in Crusade history. A new start was made with the going out of Harry and Inga-Britt Weimar in January 1962. During language study, and for general experience, they worked in cooperation with the Rev. Bob Rice and a Korean organization, the Christian Revival Fellowship, and its extensive literature program.

The invitation to C.L.C. to enter the Philippines came from about twenty missions meeting in conference in Manila, much as was the case in Pakistan. As the result of the fifty years of American occupation following the three hundred years of Spanish rule, there is an unusual combination in the Philippines of a strongly Catholic community with a real measure of freedom. The people, though religious and Catholic, are remarkably open to the gospel and approachable. Since World War II and Independence (the Philippines was the first nation to become independent after the war) there has been a large influx of new missions and missionaries, many being G. I.'s who were stationed in the islands and saw some-thing of the need.

Ray and Margaret Oram, who had opened the C.L.C. work in Japan, were asked by the Crusade to do the same in the Philippines and responded to the call. They arrived in Manila in 1957, being welcomed and helped by the Rev. Jack Frizen, of the Far Eastern Gospel Crusade, which has done much through the years to forward the C.L.C. work.

A bookstore in Manila was not the immediate need, others were handling this. Although bookstores and distribution had been stressed in the invitation, God led differently. There were practically no publications in the main languages and dialects. Shortly after the Orams' arrival in the country, the field committee of the Far Eastern Gospel Crusade asked if we could help them out with their press, as the couple who were operating it were due for furlough. It was a big responsibility for Ray who knew almost nothing about printing, but it seemed right to respond to the call, little realizing the later outcome when the Mission made a gift of all their printing equipment to the C.L.C.

As Ray stepped into the breach he was greatly helped by a national brother, Solomon Balinbin, who had already been operating the press and is still one of the mainstays of the work. A couple who had previously worked in the islands, Dick and Edith LeBar, offered to return to the field with C.L.C. to take charge of the printing and to help develop the work. Three other fine Filipino young men, Floro Matunog, Ben Naguit and Narciso Palomar, have since joined the Crusade and are actively engaged in the print shop ministry.

It soon became evident that a building would be necessary to house and adequately develop the printing program. The best solution appeared to be to purchase land and build. It was further felt that if sufficient land were available the housing for personnel could also be built and thus save a considerable outlay on rents. With these convictions strengthened through consultation with Filipino Christian businessmen, a search was made. The piece of land finally purchased proved to be unsuitable and was later sold. By now the number of workers had increased and three houses, situated together on a sort of "compound", were occupied by Crusade personnel.

Naturally, this meant quite an outlay in rent, so the search for a suitable piece of land continued.

"The Lord answered prayer in a remarkable way," says Dick LeBar. "The very compound that we were occupying, with the three dwelling houses, was offered at a price and on terms that we could now manage.

"About the same time a gift of $8,000 for a print shop building came from the Back to the Bible Broadcast in the U.S.A. When this news reached the field 'we were like them that dream.' Today a fine, new building has been added to this compound, a testimony to God's faithfulness. It is big enough to take care of future expansion and has print shop, offices and warehouse on the ground floor with living accommodation above.

"The property is very valuable, ideally located a half-block off the main north-south highway on Luzon Island. It is now in a central location in a newly-created municipality. Building is booming. Values of property are soaring; our investment is highly secure. We have improved it greatly: flood protection with staunch walls; repainting; repairing; landscaping; improvements in dwelling units."

The print shop has become thoroughly established. It is serving many missions and is pouring out life-giving literature. The 1961 output was two and one-half times as much as in 1959. The press handled over a million and three-quarters pieces of Christ-honoring literature as complete jobs—tracts, pamphlets, booklets, Bible correspondence lessons in six languages. There is much to encourage and many evidences of the literature being blessed to lives.

One of the first mission fields that C.L.C. entered was Liberia, West Africa. But the Crusade has not yet developed so strongly in Africa as on other continents. The start was made in 1946 by two W.E.C. missionaries, Herbert and Marion Congo, who volunteered to open a bookstore and literature ministry in the capital city, Monrovia. "At that time," says Ken Adams, "we had very little advice to give as to how things should be done on a mission field, but the Lord always does the unlikely and uses those who have a willing heart and spirit, and so it proved with the Congos. They obtained a large house about a block or two from the shopping area. The ground floor was turned into a nice bookstore and the rest of the building used for living quarters.

"Then came a setback. A fire destroyed not only our building in its entirety, but also five or six other properties. It was a heavy blow to a young work but we were determined to rebuild the work again. Margaret Wilson (nee Boal), later joined by Gordon and Esther Monus, continued the ministry in Monrovia and out into the country parts, particularly among the thousands of workers in the Firestone Rubber plantation and Bomi Hills mines. Now this same ministry is being carried on by Bonnie Hilton and Verna Dunrud.

"The Lord so prospered the work that Liberia became one of the first overseas centers to make a practical contribution to another overseas development. We were able to take $2,500 of their income, from their literature sales, and use it for the beginning of the work in the Philippines.

"But now comes a new challenge. A fine harbor is being built in the Lower Buchanan area which will handle about eighteen ships, whereas the harbor in Monrovia only handles about four. We feel this new center of commercial activity should have a good Christian bookstore without delay. We should not wait, but get there right in the early days of its development. To make this possible we are praying for more workers."

Senegal had a worker for some years, Vera Duke. It was not an easy ministry for one young woman among a predominately Moslem population. She lived and worked with the W.E.C. missionaries in the area, and they have continued what she began.

In Portuguese Guinea Leslie and Bessie Brierley, the W.E.C. pioneers, were importunate in their appeal to C.L.C. to open a bookstore in the capital, Bissau. "For years," they wrote, "we have sold Bibles and spiritual books, and distributed thousands of tracts over the whole country. Recently we have felt this work should be consolidated and developed to make a determined effort to reach the whole literate population of some 20,000." With the help of an initial gift of $500 from Moody Literature Mission and further help from the C.L.C., a start was made and a bookstore rented. A national worker, Ernesto Lima, felt the Lord's call to literature work and took on this new opportunity. Sales were small at first, but interest has been increased by the opening of a reading room where some have been led to Christ. The special window displays attract attention. One such was a Bible exhibition with a chained Bible on one side carrying the caption, "The prohibited Bible, fount of ignorance," and an open Bible on the other side with a background of a map of Portuguese Guinea with the caption, "The open Bible, fount of light in Guinea."

A list of literates was made and a mimeographed sheet sent out listing the Bibles and books for sale.

One day a young man came into the store who didn't seem to be the city type. On inquiry he said he had come a long way, from the Bambadina area. He had heard the gospel once and his interest was so aroused that, when the opportunity came to visit Bissau, he sought out the shop and "went off happy" with the New Testament. Another young man saw the book *We Would See Jesus* advertised and came to buy it. When asked where he had learned the gospel, he said he hadn't yet been told about it by anyone.

With the growing literacy in Portuguese Guinea the opportunities in this country are greatly increasing. Two new missionary recruits are preparing for this field and their presence will considerably strengthen the work and allow for expansion and colportage trips into the interior.

The conference of missionaries in former French West Africa have for several years invited the C.L.C. to begin a literature ministry. Dakar, Senegal, was considered as a center; but the final choice was Abidjan, the greatly expanding port of the Ivory Coast, where there is a hinterland Protestant community of about 100,000. It is the area where the Prophet Harris did his amazing work, and the Methodist Missionary Society harvested the converts into churches, and themselves welcome a new agency for the spread of Christian literature.

During 1962 plans began to crystallize for the beginning of the C.L.C. in this country. Sam and Joan Dufey, Doris Stricker and Lottie Riegg make up the team of workers now in the country and they expect to see two bookstores, in Abidjan and Bouake, established early in 1963.

These four countries, Liberia, Senegal, Portuguese Guinea and Ivory Coast. form the present bridgehead of the C.L.C. in Africa with its rapidly increasing literate populations. It is hoped that in each country the work will be strengthened and expanded and in due course other countries, such as Ghana and Sierra Leone, will be entered.

26

EPILOGUE

May the Lord preserve the C.L.C. on the road it has been taking these twenty-one years. And He will. For the C.L.C. is the living God in action, unveiling Himself through literature to a literature-hungry world, as the scripture confirms: "The words that I speak unto you, they are spirit, and they are life." I have been thrilled, page by page, in putting this little record together. I have been familiar with C.L.C. since the day of its birth. C.L.C. has been a young brother to me all these years, and many the discussions, arguments, sometimes severe differences we have had, all within the compass of an unbreakable love. But until I dug more deeply into the personal lives and experiences of those who are the C.L.C. —for C.L.C. is people, the living God through people, not an organization—I never saw so clearly the height and depth of the walk of faith, the warfare of faith, which is the life-blood of C.L.C. That is my thrill. Vision is necessary. Commission is essential. No world literature vision —no C.L.C. If to the evangelist it is "preach the gospel to every creature," to the C.L.C. it is "put the gospel-in-print into the hands of every creature."

The whole Bible and the whole Christian history attests the fact that if God's acts are to be made known to the world, it must be by people who know God' ways (Psalm 103:7). The redemption of Israel from Egypt needed a Moses who could walk and war in the Spirit, and that took some learning. The first-century churches had to have the know-how of Pentecost as well as the know-what-to-do of the Saviour's last command. The know-how of Pentecost is the revelation in experience of an exalted Christ who has taken flesh again in the members of His body and is continuing His redeeming work by them. Nothing exaggerated—the very opposite. Not some important religiosity or piousness; not necessarily brilliant human gifts and training; not some automated, computer-style organization; but just God's nobodies, simple men and women, often unlikely men and women, who are taken through a Moses-process of self-exposure, self-humiliation, and then self-liberation as common bushes aflame with God.

These chapters are full of such. Once more, that is my thrill and my reward in writing this. C.L.C. is not a mechanical modern factory with its unending production lines. Each development of the work is an original, because each is a person who is the living God in human clothing: "The Father that dwelleth in Me doeth the works"; "the Spirit of the Lord clothed Himself with Gideon"; "yet not I but the grace of God which was with me." Therefore, each testimony is equally a romance, a romance of faith. The human element sticks out all over the place, and is meant to: the fears, shrinkings, repulsions, perplexities; the weaknesses, the poverty, the impossibility, the constantly glaring contrasts between actual appearances and high-sounding objectives; and then—the gradual uprising of the building of God not made with hands, the work really done, the business efficiency; the books and pamphlets procured, printed, published and outpoured by the tens of millions; the finances supplied (always only just enough!) the necessary buildings and bookmobiles, supremely the dedicated personnel, the countries entered.

Yet through it all, the weakness and foolishness of faith is never to be replaced by the apparent strength and wisdom of human security and organization. Soren Kierkegaard, that great exponent of the paradox of faith, well said: "Spiritual existence is not easy; the believer constantly lies upon the deep, has 70,000 fathoms of water underneath him. However long he lies out there, that does not mean that he gradually comes to lie on land and stretch himself. He may become calmer, more experienced, find a security that loves jesting and a happy mind, but to his last instant he lies upon a depth of 70,000 fathoms of water."

The vision remains. The C.L.C. and all literature missionaries would say the surface is hardly scratched yet. The burden still presses and will to the end of time until Christ in person takes over. Increase, increase, increase must be the password. On, on, on! Go, go, go! "Forgetting those things that are behind, we press toward the mark." If C.L.C. is this big in twenty-one years, the next twenty-one must see a four-fold increase. National literature missionaries must so arise and take over in spirit—and C.L.C. has done well in this respect already—that the sense of this being an agency with "Western home bases and foreign fields" will have disappeared, and the whole world become a chain of cooperating literature home bases and headquarters, each with its total national outreach. Christ-centered literature by the whole church to the whole world, and by all Christ-centered, Bible-centered agencies that God calls into being. Amen. So be it. Even so come Lord Jesus, by literature, by the printed word, till You come in person.